Copyright: UKCS 235758

First published June 2007

Published by Harman Usher/Sally Parker

ISBN: 0-9548561-5-5

Contents

INTRODUCTION

The definitive guide sets out to clearly define the purpose of the Résumé/Curriculum Vitae in today's society.

Having worked for private training companies sub-contracted to the Employment Services, the author has contacted, liaised with and listened to hundreds of employers, human resources, personnel managers, recruitment agencies, colleges and training providers. Above all else one thing has become very apparent, the need for a complete overhaul and re-evaluation of the modern Résumé/CV

Ninety six percent of all employers contacted agree that the Résumé/CV is generally a poorly constructed, visually ineffective, boring and often fictitious document.

With rapid advancement in all areas of industry and every day life it is time to make changes and review the most basic employment tool, the Résumé/Curriculum Vitae.

The guide answers questions, provides examples and most importantly satisfies the requirements of potential employers.

HOW IMPORTANT IS A RÉSUMÉ/CV

Over the past few years it would be fair to say that the importance of a Résumé/CV has greatly diminished. In the past a CV could be expected to get you the interview, at the present time the CV in most instances will now only get you an application form.

Hardly a surprising development when one considers that the CV is an unsigned and consequently unproven document. Past experience has shown that many a Résumé/CV has been used to obtain employment in professions where qualifications and experience are vital, for example:

The gentleman practising medicine for eight years, his CV claimed he had gained medical qualifications in Nairobi, Kenya. The qualification turned out to be fictitious, as a result of investigation after a patient died because of his bad diagnosis.

With many more examples of bogus achievements and qualifications, employers are rarely prepared to accept these unsigned documents entirely on face value.

However, the Résumé/CV is still a most useful tool, it can be sent out on a speculative basis accompanied by a covering letter, used as a prompt when completing application forms and providing a quick overview to potential employers when responding to an advertised vacancy.

CV OR RÉSUMÉ

It is important to determine which format is most suited to your employment needs and requirements. In the United Kingdom the current trend leans toward the American style Résumé, which in essence is a shortened version of the European Curriculum Vitae. The Résumé is generally one or two pages in length providing an overview rather than the lengthier "Path of Life" as favoured in Europe.

VISUAL IMPACT

As in life first impressions often count. If your Résumé/CV is poorly laid out and causes potential employers to spend time searching for information, they are less likely to read it.

Reverse the role, put yourself in the position of the potential employer. You have advertised a popular job and have received dozens of applications, bearing in mind that on average most employers spend little more than twenty seconds scanning your Résumé/CV, those lacking initial impact are going to be easily passed over.

You may be the perfect choice for the job but because your CV is poorly structured you fail at the first hurdle.

The colour and grade of paper used can also be an important consideration, first impressions can count, a well laid out CV/ Résumé on a good quality paper can enhance the 'Reader appeal', getting you noticed. When choosing a colour, ensure that it is neither to dark or to bold, pastels or plain white are usually the most effective.

STARTING OUT

PERSONAL DETAILS

The Curriculum Vitae or Résumé should always start with your name. There is absolutely no point in stating the obvious by saying this is the CV of: Your name should be followed by your address including a post/zip code, which in turn is followed by contact telephone number details, a mobile number could also be useful. Finally e-mail address if you have one.

Example:

MARTIN GREEN
1734 Wimbley Gardens
Poole BH17 4LP
Tel: 01202 889900   Mobile: 01772 678900
E-mail: martingreen@aol.com.

The authors preferred style is to bold and capitalise the name only. This makes it reader friendly without using line spacing, which may help when looking to condense longer documents.

You will notice that no age, date of birth, ethnicity or marital status is shown, information asked for on an application form but not volunteered on a CV

FONT STYLE

Choosing a font style is down to the individual, it should be appealing to the eye, not overpowering or difficult to read.

Most standard résumés are prepared using Times New Roman or Ariel, although the latter can appear a little harsh on detailed documents. Ariel spacing is greater than Times New Roman, which might be another consideration if trying to condense information onto a maximum of two pages.

Times New Roman strikes a happy balance between standard and bolded type, thus giving a professional, easy to read appearance.

Having chosen your font style it is strongly recommended not to incorporate other styles. Many CVs/Résumés use script or even italics to draw attention to certain aspects or details. The overall result often detracts rather than enhances the visual impact.

SIZE OF TYPE/FONT

When choosing a font size for the compilation of a short version CV/Résumé, it is important to remember that you will only be using a maximum of two pages. If you have an extensive history of employment you may need to conserve space, therefore you would need to use a font size, which would not be too small to read or make your CV look too busy, or too large and lose space.

Finding the font size that best suits you is a matter of trial and error. The favoured font size by the author is 11 point throughout the CV. It is never advisable to fluctuate in size as this could make the CV appear to be disjointed.

HEADINGS

The use of headings can greatly increase the visual impact of the Résumé/CV, a potential employer can seek out the section of information relevant to him. Once again the type of heading used is best chosen by the individual, but remember that fancy designed headings can detract from content.

The following headings are dealt with in detail and are used to paint the overall picture required by most employers.

SKILLS PROFILE

EMPLOYMENT HISTORY

EDUCATION

ACHIEVEMENTS AND ADDITIONAL TRAINING EXPERIENCE

LEISURE INTERESTS

ADDITIONAL INFORMATION

PROFILES

What is a profile and is it really necessary?

The purpose of a profile is to present a focused statement to a potential employer. The type of profile used would be dependent upon the individuals past work or educational background.

For example, the school leaver has no work experience and would therefore rely heavily upon a personal profile followed by academic achievements.

The experienced individual has developed a wealth of transferable skills and would therefore present a "skills profile" followed by employment history.

The individual seeking a return to employment after a substantial career break would present a soft skills profile, which, would indicate past experiences and personal attributes in a balanced format, followed by an explanation for the break and the employment history.

This particular format is dealt with in more detail quite separately in a later chapter.

THE PERSONAL PROFILE

This style of profile is generally used to give an overview of individual qualities and is often the preferred format of schools and colleges. Apart from the paper round, occasional evening or weekend job, few school leavers have experience of employment. Although these part time jobs can demonstrate a desire to achieve individual goals, few employers would feel that there are any developed transferable skills rather than personal attributes.

Typical examples of personal profiles:

An enthusiastic young man eager to gain retail experience, hard working, diligent and reliable, prepared to undertake any available training.
Keen, conscientious, hard working and reliable person. I am a good time keeper and enjoy meeting people. I can adapt to any environment and would like to use my skills to contribute positively to any work situation.

I am punctual, reliable and work well under pressure, either as part of a team or alone, I am straight forward and positive in my approach to work.

THE SKILLS PROFILE

The skills profile provides a focused overview, an "Attention Getter" laying out The Five Point System.

1. Experience

2. Responsibilities

3. Additional Skills

4. Personal Attributes

5. Direction

The profile should be short, concise and interesting. Remembering that the Résumé/CV will only receive a twenty-second glance, a very short time to get someone's attention and hold it.

The authors preferred lay out for the skills profile is to accentuate the overall impact by the use of bullet points and bolding. When a Résumé/CV is viewed the eye should be drawn to the skills profile, the information the employer wants to know. Always remember that if the potential employer has to hunt for information your Résumé/CV is more likely to be passed over.

THE FIVE POINT SYSTEM

EXPERIENCE

The first point is the initial attention grabber showing the potential employer what experience you have, doing what!

Examples:

- More than twenty years experience as a fully qualified motor vehicle technician.

- An experienced I.T. manager, technically and commercially qualified

- A highly experienced senior contracts manager.

- More than twelve years business management/sales marketing experience with extensive international exposure.

- Fifteen years experience working within a variety of industry including retail, catering, administration and sales.

- A well educated (Degree level) professional with extensive experience of design, development and testing within the electronics industry.

RESPONSIBILITIES

The second point highlights the main responsibilities within your present or past employment, often called "key skills", the buying signals, which indicate to a potential employer, your suitability for the position applied for.

Examples:

- Responsible for the day-to-day running of a busy workshop, supervising mechanics, liaising with customers, stock management and security.

- Responsible for developing I.T. strategies, managing multiple projects such as Lan/Wan roll out across multiple sites.

- Fully conversant with the principles of project management, business analysis and networking.

- Commercially astute professional with a proven track record of achieving and surpassing targets.

- Responsible for the daily running of retail outlets, staff training, quality controls, customer services, displays and promotions.

- Designing programmable logic controllers and servo systems, writing and testing plc programmes and motion control software.

ADDITIONAL SKILLS

The third point offers additional skills drawn from both current and past employment history. These skills offer employers additional "buying signals", often referred to as soft skills.

Examples:

- Further experiences include trouble shooting down to component level, preparing quotes, basic bookkeeping and administration.

- Additional responsibilities have included board presentations, generating cost v benefit v risk analysis, developing financial and technical projections.

- Achieving and surpassing targets, developing and implementing winning marketing strategies.

- A highly motivated decision maker capable of innovative planning leading to year on year growth.

- Further experience of cash handling, displays, window dressing, operating EPOS tills, stock rotation and promotions.

- Commissioning and faultfinding, training service engineers, producing circuit diagrams using CAD.

PERSONAL ATTRIBUTES

Point number four is often confused with key skills. Personal attributes are the qualities that others would use to describe you. Key skills are transferable responsibilities. Avoid such words such as honest, reliable, conscientious, trustworthy. Most employers will decide for themselves on these points. Instead, give useful information that will match your abilities.

Examples:

- An effective team player used to working within demanding environments where initiative and logic are prime requisites.

- An effective presenter, self-motivated with proven business, team management, customer facing and leadership skills.

- Able to effectively prioritise workloads, demonstrating first class communication skills and a keen eye for detail.

- Fully literate in PC based business applications, reactive to change, pro-active and performance driven.

- Able to work on own initiative or as part of a team, demonstrating well-proven communication and customer care skills.

- Used to working to exacting schedules within high-pressure environments. Able to effectively prioritise workloads, demonstrating both initiative and logic.

DIRECTION

The fifth point of the skills profile would indicate the type of work being sought or the career path being pursued.

Examples:

- Ideally seeking a position where skills and experiences within the automotive industry could be drawn upon.

- Ideally placed for a senior appointment within commercial I.T./project management.

- Keen to exploit above key skills within project/contract management or similar demanding work environment.

- Seeking to enhance a client led organisation with fresh impetus and inspired support.

- Seeking a position where above skills and experiences could be drawn upon and further developed.

- Seeking to draw upon above key skills as a test engineer or similar role.

EXTENDING OR SHORTENING PROFILES

Although the "five point" system is favoured for its construction, it is not set in concrete. It is sometimes expanded into six or more points, but, bear in mind the more points you include the harder it becomes to maintain the attention of the reader.

By shortening the points to four or less you are reducing your overall impact by the omission of "buying signals", or even the softer "personal attributes". Therefore the overall picture would not necessarily be complete.

EMPLOYMENT HISTORY

The employment history would normally follow on from the skills profile. You have already told the potential employer what your skills are, now he wants to know about your experience "doing what for whom".

You have grabbed the reader's attention by focusing them on your skills profile, it is now important to lay out your employment history in as easy to read format as possible. Always remember that searching for information detracts from impact.

The first point of interest would normally be the date and length of employment. It is generally recommended to only show years rather than days and months.

Example:

2005-2007

If we look again at the purpose of the Résumé/CV, it is usually to get you an application form, which may then ask for more specific dates.

The date should be displayed on the left side, it is relevant information to the potential employer. Many a Résumé/CV places dates on the right, which detracts from ease of reading and can create a question in the reader's mind, why is attention being drawn away from the date? Are you trying to disguise a period of unemployment?

Reading from left to right the date would be followed by job title, which, in turn would be followed by the company name and location. The following examples will demonstrate ease of reading, the potential employer can see at a glance i.e. when you worked, what you did and where.

2005-2007   Retail Assistant
            Candy Box, Bournemouth, Dorset.

If you now use bold to highlight the date and position you add to the visual impact without detracting from the profile. Too much bolding would draw the eye away from the initial attention grabber, the important details are "when and what", rather than for whom.

Example:

2005-2007 Retail Assistant
Candy Box, Bournemouth, Dorset.

Having set out the date, position, company name and location, it is necessary to give a brief summary of responsibilities or duties. Many a Résumé/CV losses impact by the use of numerous bullet points and far too much information. Keep it brief and to the point, you will be given ample opportunity to expand on your responsibilities and experiences at the interview stage.

Examples:

2005-2007 Retail Assistant
Candy Box, Bournemouth, Dorset.
Responsible for assisting with the day-to-day running of a busy retail outlet including direct customer liaison, cash handling, stock rotation, displays and window dressing.

2001-2005 Administrator
Parker Secretarial, Poole, Dorset.
Carrying out all administrative duties including typing, filing, collating, data entry, preparing correspondence and answering telephones.

2000-2001 Secretary/Receptionist
Barns Recruitment, Poole, Dorset.
Working as a secretary on a short-term agency contract including dealing with customer enquiries and diary management.

The examples shown are short, informative and relevant. Every employer will know that you would have done far more than you have mentioned.

Not all professions can be so neatly summarised into two or three lines. The microbiologist, the industrial chemist, the development engineer and many, many more would have extensive project, research, development and specialist skills. In these instances it is often advisable to prepare a separate summary or portfolio detailing achievements rather than condensing them.

HOW MUCH EMPLOYMENT HISTORY

It is advisable to limit your employment history details to a maximum of twenty years. Longer periods than this can place too much emphasis on age, which, despite all rhetoric can still be a great barrier to employment.

In a lot of cases it can often be advantageous to restrict the employment history to ten years, or even as little as five, especially when many different short term jobs have been undertaken. It can also assist in drawing any attention away from previous periods of unemployment, especially long term; in these instances it can be very useful to use a career summary.

CAREER SUMMARY

A career summary can often be used to indicate early employment or to highlight other work experiences prior to a change in career direction.

Example:

1994-2006 Office Manager
> Birchfield Services, Bournemouth, Dorset.
> Responsible for the supervision and training of twelve administrative staff, processing insurance, investment and mortgage applications, liaising with customers, monitoring data controls and compliance with regulatory issues.

CAREER SUMMARY

Additional experiences include working within the production, stores and engineering sectors with responsibility for stock management, the production of "one off" machine components, goods inward, shipping and invoicing.

The example demonstrates ten years experience of office management, followed by the career summary, which indicates an unspecified period working in other industries. A few of the important skills have been mentioned which may well be additional points of interest to a potential employer.

EDUCATION

When compiling Résumé/CVs some of the most frequently asked questions pertain to the subject of education.

Examples:

(A)   How far back should I go?

(B)   I changed school several times.

(C)   My school closed down, should I mention it?

(D)   I did not gain any qualifications.

(E)   It has been many years since I left school.

To resolve these questions many hundreds of employers were contacted to express their views. Although opinions vary the majority of employers agree to the following:

THE SCHOOL LEAVER

If leaving school and seeking work it would be beneficial to show individual subjects and grades achieved.

i.e.   History   GCSE   Grade A
       Maths   GCSE   Grade C
       English   GCSE   Grade B
       Science   GCSE   Grade B

However, it should also be noted that not everyone leaves school with passes or qualifications.

In the United Kingdom mainstream secondary education commences at the age of eleven and ends at the age of sixteen, unless continuing on to sixth form for a further year. Common standards for education are set, currently the general certificate of education (GCSE) is the standard.

If you are about to leave school without gaining any qualifications, it is perfectly acceptable to state that you are educated to GCSE standard in all core subjects. You are not claiming to have GCSE's but merely educated to that standard.

THE PERSON WITH WORK EXPERIENCE

Having left school and worked, your secondary education is far less relevant as you will have gained experience as well as transferable skills "Buying signals".

If you have many years of work experience, there would be little point in mentioning what grades you achieved, even if you could remember them. If you returned to school tomorrow to re-sit those long forgotten examinations you would probably fail them miserably! Employers understand this, therefore, little consideration is given.

One of the best ways found to answer the questions posed would be to show only the last school attended, prior to commencing employment.

Example:

Grange Secondary, Poole, Dorset.

Farnby Comprehensive, Bournemouth, Dorset.

Gladstone Grammar, Blandford, Dorset.

Having given the name and location of the school attended, all that would be of any further practical use would be to indicate if you have numeracy and literacy skills.

Example:

Educated to GCSE standard in all core subjects including Maths and English.

GCSE in six subjects including Maths and English

Earlier education, (prior to GCSE) would be the GCE or CSE standard, the same instruction applies, merely total up your passes or state that you were educated to GCE standard.

DATES

When preparing the education section, unless you are a recent school leaver, it is not necessary to show dates. If you have an extended employment history then showing dates of education may draw attention to age, which may not be desirable.

FURTHER EDUCATION

If after leaving secondary school and going on to college to gain 'A' levels, this could also be included under the heading of education. If returning to college after a period of employment it would fall in to the next section of the CV, achievements and additional training experience.

UNIVERSITY

Attendance at a university is not part of the mainstream general education, more a chosen field of subjects. Qualifications and university attended would also come under the next heading of achievements.

COMBINATION

In some instances it maybe preferable to combine this section and the next, so instead of showing education separately it blends with achievements and additional training experiences. The heading would then appear as simply:

Education and Achievements

This particular heading is often favoured when there is extensive employment history in specialised fields or higher academic achievements. With masters degrees or higher there is little interest in mainstream or secondary school details.

ACHIEVEMENTS AND ADDITIONAL TRAINING EXPERIENCE

This section provides the potential employer with skills information relating to all further qualifications and achievements since leaving school. If you have made a return to education or attended night school, here is the opportunity to mention it. If you have participated in skills development courses, gained computer skills or attended seminars, here is your chance to further impress employers.

Always remember that no matter what type of work you have previously done, you will have gained a wealth of transferable skills. You will have received instruction on how to do the job and in most positions some ongoing training. This ongoing training could encompass health and safety, fire prevention, use of new equipment, customer care or just about anything. This type of instruction would usually fall under the heading of in-house training.

It is important to find the right balance when listing achievements, if your qualifications and achievements far exceed the job requirements you will be very unlikely to land the job. Many a job applicant has lost out because they were considered to be over qualified for the position applied for.

Examples:

ACHIEVEMENTS AND ADDITIONAL TRAINIING EXPERIENCE

BSc (HONs) Reading Physics and Technology of Electronics
Finance for Non-Financial Managers and Bookkeeping
Various Sales and Marketing Courses
Use of Computers in Industry

BSc (HONs) – Building Technology/Construction
Risk Management (Institute of Occupational H&S)
NEBOSH General Certificate
CDM Planning Supervisors Course
BS1 Quality Assurance Auditors Course
ISO 9001 Implementation Course
First Aid, Fire Fighting and Fire Safety Course

B-Tech (equivalent) - Office Management
In-House Training
Communication Techniques – Customer Care
Customer Services – Stock Management – Data Entry
Sale Techniques – Administrative Procedures
Security Protocols – Health & Safety.

LEISURE INTERESTS

What is the purpose of leisure interests when applying for employment and what do employers look for? Another of those frequently asked questions.

Over the last few years we have seen many changes occur within the employment sector. More and more companies are dispensing with their in-house personnel managers, instead of these managers the companies are farming out their recruitment requirements to agencies specialising in human resources.

Leisure interests were always targeted by a well-trained personnel manager as a first question, "ice breaker" at interview.

Your leisure interests can also highlight additional buying signals or reinforce attributes. If you are a member of a club, participate in competitions or play a team game, you will also be showing communication and team skills. If you enjoy completing crosswords, entering into quizzes, play chess or scrabble you are also showing that you enjoy a challenge and use your brainpower. In the work place you have the ability to show initiative.

If you have a very unusual interest you could even influence the very first question at interview.

When setting out leisure interests we need to make it as interesting as possible, avoid; reading, music, walking etc., unless you expand, specify what you read or the type of music you enjoy listening to.

Example:

Enjoy reading a wide range of literature, especially horror stories, a favourite author being Stephen King.

Listening to 60's, 70's and classical music.

Going for long countryside walks for the pleasure of being outdoors.

The above examples have expanded on the bland walking, reading and music by adding points of interest. Many a job has been landed because of similar interests.

It would also be advisable to avoid controversial issues such as politics, hunting and gun sports. Religious beliefs or convictions should also be avoided, unless of course you are applying for a clerical position.

Never try to over impress a potential employer, keep your interests factual, you can be sure that if you claim an interest there will always be someone else who does it.

The classical example would be the young man who attended interview and gained employment as an office assistant. His CV and application form showed his leisure interests to be football, skydiving and jogging. Several weeks after commencing the job he was summoned to the manger's office, the manager informed him that he was in fact the chairman for the local skydiving association, the company would be participating in a charity skydiving event. A very uncomfortable position for the young man especially when he had never been more than two feet off the ground!

Sometimes if a person is unemployed they may no longer have the same interests as when they were working, once they start working again the hobbies or interests are resumed, show them as your interests, they are merely on hold.

Avoid showing too many activities, you could appear to be too busy to work. In most instances four activities should be sufficient.

Many people avoid showing that they enjoy ski-ing, diving, motor racing and other possible hazardous sports, purely out of the belief that employers would consider them to be more at risk from injury, thus keeping them away from work. It is fair to say that a few employers believed this to be the case but the major majority stated that it would not be a consideration.

ADDITIONAL INFORMATION

This section is not obligatory but if shown should only include relevant information. So what is relevant?

Many CVs/Résumés include several lines of repetitive information "waffle", re-stating objectives and experiences.
Relevant information such as:

"Clean Current Driving Licence"

"Fluent French – written and spoken"

"British Sign Language"

These points maybe of interest to a potential employer, the position applied for may include the use of a company car. The ability to communicate in another language or communicate using sign language might also be of benefit.

Such Points As:

In good health
Date of Birth
Married with children
Non-smoker

Are of little importance, it is usually accepted that you will be reasonably fit or you would not be applying for the position. A determination as to your state of health and ability will be determined at the application form stage or interview. It is also advisable not to include your age or date of birth, this information can send the wrong signal, you could be passed over at the first hurdle because you are considered too old or young.

In the United Kingdom smoking is now considered to be anti-social, more and more work places insist on a non-smoking policy. If you can't smoke at work why mention that you are a non-smoker.

REFERENCES

Never include your references on a CV or Résumé. Advise potential employers "references are available upon request".

By including your references on your Résumé/CV you are giving the opportunity to everyone who reads it to contact them. Your referees could soon tire of this, especially if you have sent out many CVs' on a speculative approach.

EMPLOYMENT GAPS

Short breaks in employment are not usually considered a problem, few people leave a job and fall straight into another.

As the period of unemployment lengthens, it begins to become a serious barrier, long-term unemployment of perhaps a year or more can become the major barrier to gaining employment.

In the United Kingdom a stigma has been attached to the word 'Unemployed'. This is due in part to the benefits culture that has developed among a proportion of the long term "Professionally" unemployed. Persons who are content to rely solely on the welfare state in the misguided belief that it is their right not to work.

As a result of this, if you have been out of work for a long period of time, potential employers may not even consider you, in the belief that you have 'Got out of the routine of working'. The next question they would ask is "Why are you unemployed?" As time goes by this can become very difficult to answer.

Many a CV/Résumé states "Actively seeking work" during periods of unemployment, which after a year is a contradiction. If you had been actively seeking you would have found something.

There are of course many reasons for not working, which are readily accepted by potential employers.

Examples:

The lone parent who has taken time out from employment to raise a family. Most employers would recognise that raising a family is in itself a full time job.

Recovery from an illness or accident.

Career break to undertake further education or attend courses to develop new skills for a change in career direction.

Time out as a carer.

CLOSING THE GAP

Periods of long-term unemployment can be overcome in several ways, if you have undertaken any form of voluntary work, helping out in a charity shop, becoming involved in community projects, assisting the elderly or fund raising. These are just a few of the examples of how you could have been using your time.

Most employers would appreciate that although the voluntary work may be totally unrelated to either the position, or type of work you are applying for, you are demonstrating that you have been doing something with your time. You have kept yourself busy and therefore may not have fallen out of the routine of working.

Another option chosen to close down long periods of unemployment by some individuals is to show that they have been self-employed.

Examples:

2004-2006 Maintenance Operative.
Self-employed, Bournemouth, Dorset.
Carrying out general property maintenance within the private sector, including painting, decorating and new build.

2002-2004 Mobile Vehicle Mechanic.
M & J Mobile Services, Bournemouth, Dorset.
Proprietor and operator of a small company specialising in the repair and maintenance of vehicles.

The two examples show a two-year period of self-employment. In truth the individuals are disguising periods of unemployment which, they could be called upon at the interview stage to further expand upon. Their use of the word self-employed is solely based on the definition of the word 'Employ', which means 'Use'. Therefore they are using themselves. Before embarking on this course of action be sure you can substantiate it when called upon to do so.

A good solution to the problem of long gaps in employment is to once again revert back to the 'career summary'. With this type of summary dates are specifically avoided.

Example:

CAREER SUMMARY

Employment history would include working within a variety of industry in a sub contracted role, including construction, building reservoirs, laying pipes for drainage and building utilities. Additional work at the Worth Air Base installing cladding for hangers, laying pipes for drainage and building utilities. Working as an erector for Can-O-Ducts of Reading, installing ducting for air conditioning units within offices, factory units and large shopping complexes. Liaising with architects and site personnel, reading blueprints, following rigid Health and Safety guidelines. Further experiences include working as a storeman with Ford Motor Company, commencing as a parts stacker for shipment and progressing to storeman/checker with responsibility for stock management. Ensuring parts were delivered within exacting time schedules, liaising with department heads and senior management.

The example shown does not specify dates of employment but offers a detailed overview of responsibilities. There could quite easily be long periods of unemployment concealed within the summary, but by presenting it in a flowing format, the emphasis is drawn away from specific dates.

CONCLUSION

The definitive guide has taken you through a step by step guide for the compilation of your short version curriculum vitae/résumé, the style that is popular amongst employers within the United Kingdom and United States job markets. However in conclusion it should also be stated that there are many presentation styles, a graphic designer may use a background theme to highlight his expertise, a record producer might construct his resume around a disc. Whatever style you choose always ensure that you get the relevant information across, after all, time is money to most employers, the quicker they see what you have to offer them the better.

The following profile and résumé examples may help you in the construction of your personal 'Selling document'.

EXAMPLES OF SKILLS PROFILES

- A experienced clerical administrator familiar with all systems and procedures of a busy office environment.
- Responsibilities include direct customer liaising, data entry, customer services, filing, collating, faxing, report writing, dealing with confidential information and cash handling.
- Further experience teaching English as a second language in Swedish schools.
- Able to work in high-pressure environments demonstrating well-proven communication and customer care skills along with the ability to effectively prioritise workloads.
- Ideally seeking an office based administrative or similar position where above skills and experiences could be drawn upon and further expanded.

- More than twenty years sales/marketing experience with extensive national exposure.
- Commercially astute professional with a proven track record of achieving and surpassing targets, developing, implementing and harvesting winning marketing strategies.
- Highly motivated decision maker capable of innovative planning leading to year on year growth.
- Ideally suited to exploiting above key skills within sales/marketing or similar demanding work environment.

- More than twenty years 'Hands on' experience gained within the commercial sector refurbishing/servicing catering equipment and general maintenance.
- Responsible for supervision and training of new employees, on-site installations, repairs and overhauls of both new and used catering equipment.
- Further experiences include liaising with customers, cash handling and banking, diagnostics, plumbing, gas fitting, stock controls and maintenance procedures.
- An effective team member capable of demonstrating individual initiative, able to effectively prioritise workloads with a keen eye for detail.
- Seeking a position where above skills and experiences could be drawn upon, utilised and further developed.

- A highly motivated individual with three years work experience including painting, decorating and gardening.
- Responsible for carrying out a wide range of general property maintenance for private sector clients including priming, painting, filling and snagging.
- Further experience working within a busy garden centre, liaising with customers, advising on products, cultivating, cash handling, stock controls and security.
- An effective team member capable of working on own initiative, demonstrating good communication and customer care skills.
- Preferred work areas would include postal work or painting/decorating where above skills and experiences could be drawn upon and further developed.

- An enthusiastic individual with a wealth of 'Hands on' experience including catering and warehousing.
- Responsible for carrying out all rear of house duties within busy hotel and catering establishments.
- Further experience of stores, goods inwards, collation of orders, customer liaison, stock controls and operating EPOS systems.
- An effective team player able to work on own initiative, demonstrating a keen eye for detail and the ability to effectively prioritise.
- Ideally seeking a position where catering skills and experiences could be drawn upon and further expanded.

- More than ten years experience working within a variety of industry including production, entertainment and hospitality.
- Responsible for overseeing day-to-day operations including staff supervision, direct customer liaison, stock management, quality controls, cash handling and banking.
- Further experiences include security (Key holder), dealing with problems and complaints, property maintenance and the installation of conservatories.
- Used to working within high-pressure environments with the ability to effectively prioritise workloads, demonstrating well-developed communication and customer care skills.
- Ideally seeking a position within the security industry where above skills and experiences could be drawn upon and further developed.

- A highly experienced manager with particular expertise dealing with FMCG's.
- Interviewed, appraised, trained and monitored staff throughout career.
- Confident, caring, efficient with a distinctly 'Hands on' management style, innovative and imaginative in approach to marketing, promotions and shop displays.
- Winner of 'Shop of the month' (23 out of 24 months).
- Reactive to change, proactive to challenge and performance driven.
- Ideally seeking a managerial position where above skills and experiences could be drawn upon and further expanded.

- An enthusiastic individual with extensive childcare experience.
- Responsible for supervising children between the ages of four to twelve in after school club environments.
- Organising a wide range of activities, supervising staff, arranging day trips, minibus driving, liaising with parents and relevant bodies.
- An effective team player capable of working on own initiative, demonstrating well-proven communication and care skills.
- Ideally seeking a childcare/classroom assistant or similar role where above experiences could be drawn upon and further expanded.

- A well educated (Degree level) professional with extensive experience of design, development and testing within the electronics industry.
- Designing programmable logic controllers and servo systems, ensuring EMC compliance, writing and testing PLC programmes and motion control software.
- Commissioning and fault finding down to component level, training service engineers and producing circuit diagrams using CAD.
- Used to working to exacting schedules within high-pressure environments. Able to effectively prioritise workloads demonstrating both initiative and logic.
- Seeking to draw upon above key skills as a test engineer or similar role.

- More than twenty years experience working within the hospitality sector.
- Responsible for the day-to-day running of busy establishments, supervising and training staff, stock management and direct customer liaison.
- Further experiences include cash handling, customer services, promotions, displays, advertising, administration and basic bookkeeping.
- Used to working within high-pressure environments where initiative and logic are prime requisites, demonstrating well-proven communication and customer care skills.
- Ideally seeking a position where 'People skills' could be drawn upon and further expanded.

- An enthusiastic individual with extensive stores/warehousing experience.
- Responsible for the day-to-day running of busy warehouse environments, staff training and supervision, goods inwards and administration.
- Further experiences include direct customer liaison, order processing, displays, promotions and security protocols (Key holder).
- An effective team player capable of using individual initiative, demonstrating well-proven communication, time management and customer care skills.
- Ideally seeking a position where stores/warehouse skills and experiences could be drawn upon and further expanded.

- More than twenty years experience working within a variety of industry including distance and multi-drop driving.
- Responsible for the collection, welfare and safety of school children, vehicle upkeep, liaising with parents and teachers.
- Further experiences include delivery of mail packages, cash handling, supervision and training, customer services, security, quality controls, basic bookkeeping and general administration.
- Well-proven communication and customer care skills, able to work within high-pressure environments demonstrating initiative and the ability to effectively prioritise.
- Ideally seeking a customer facing role within the retail/shop environment occasionally delivering goods if required.

- Recent experience as an Employment Advisor with particular interest in self-employment strategies.
- Skills include identifying employment barriers and providing solutions towards career direction and development.
- Responsibilities have included management and supervision of staff, training and overall security for property and personal data.
- Computer literate, able to work in high-pressure environments where initiative and logic are essential tools. Highly motivated, methodical, paying great attention to detail.
- Well placed to continue developing career, undertaking further training to enhance skills base.

- An experienced IT manager, technically and commercially qualified, fully conversant with the principles of project management, business analysis and networking.
- Responsible for developing and deploying IT strategies, managing multiple projects such as LAN/WAN rollout across multiple sites, controlling budgets, negotiating contracts and administering the IT department including purchasing and recruitment.
- Further responsibilities included board presentations, generating cost v benefit v risk analysis, developing financial and technical projections, leading in-house seminars and writing functional specifications mainly within SME's in the private sector.
- Ideally placed for a senior appointment within commercial IT/project management and willing to commute or relocate.

- An enthusiastic individual with a wealth of classroom support and customer facing experience.
- Assisting in the day-to-day running of busy primary school classrooms, liaising with teachers, monitoring activities and children's learning.
- Further experiences include office administration, data entry, collating, report writing, diary management, cash handling and security.
- An effective team player capable of working on own initiative, demonstrating well-proven communication and customer care skills.
- Ideally seeking a position, preferably with a school environment, where above skills and experiences could be drawn upon and further expanded.

- More than twenty years experience as a fibreglass laminator.
- Responsible for the manufacture and development of moldings/molds used within the automotive, boating and commercial sectors.
- Further experiences include staff supervision and training, stock management, set-up and establishment of new facilities, direct customer liaison, quality controls and security.
- An effective team player capable of working on own initiative, demonstrating well-proven communication skills and a keen eye for detail.
- Ideally seeking a position where wide range of skills and experiences could be drawn upon and utilised.

- An enthusiastic individual having recently completed a reception training and switchboard operations course.
- Responsible for assisting within busy classroom environments including administration, teacher support, monitoring children and giving swimming lessons.
- Further experience within the production sector carrying out a wide range of invisible repairs to garments.
- Able to work on own initiative or as part of a team, demonstrating first class communication skills and the ability to effectively prioritise.
- Ideally seeking a position where reception skills could be drawn upon and further developed.

- An enthusiastic highly motivated individual with retail and customer facing experience.
- Responsible for assisting with the day-to-day running of busy retail outlets, serving customers, operating tills, cash handling. Stock controls and security.
- Further experiences include voluntary work as a parent helper and animal welfare assistant with the RSPCA.
- Used to working on own initiative or as part of a team, demonstrating excellent communication and customer care skills along with the ability to effectively prioritise workloads.
- Ideally seeking a position where retail skills and experiences could be drawn upon and further developed.

- More than twenty years supervisory and management experience gained within technical sales and call centre environments.
- Responsible for the day-to-day management of twenty plus staff, direct customer liaison, preparing detailed instructions for the manufacture of goods.
- Further experience of quality controls, customer services, stock management, scheduling, pricing, preparing exhibitions and displays, advising on all aspects of debt recovery.
- Well-proven communication and customer care skills, able to work on own initiative or as part of a team demonstrating the ability to effectively prioritise.
- Ideally seeking an office based position where above skills and experiences could be drawn upon and further developed.

- A highly motivated individual with a wealth of 'Hands on' experience including general maintenance, landscaping and warehousing.
- Responsible for the overall upkeep of school properties, painting, decorating, gardening, snagging and emergency repairs.
- Further experience of warehousing, forestry and landscaping, operating a wide range of equipment including reach and counterbalance forklifts.
- Used to working on own initiative or within a team, demonstrating a keen eye for detail and the ability to effectively prioritise.
- Ideally seeking a position where above skills and experiences, preferably within the maintenance sector, could be drawn upon and further developed.

- More than twenty years experience of HGV driving and stores management.
- Responsible for operating HGV class 1 vehicles, delivering a wide range of products throughout both Europe and the United Kingdom.
- Further experiences include the day-to-day running of busy store/warehouses, operating forklifts, goods inwards, security and direct customer liaison.
- Used to working on own initiative demonstrating first class communication skills and the ability to effectively prioritise workloads.

- An experienced well qualified (Degree level) Civil Engineer.
- Responsible for working on a wide range of contracts including new-build, reconstruction and water projects.
- Further experience setting out drainage, office blocks and car parks.
- Used to working in environments where initiative, logic and a keen eye for detail are prime requisites.
- Seeking a position within civil engineering where skills and experiences could be drawn upon and further expanded.

- More than twenty years groundwork experience working on a wide range of road building contracts.
- Responsible for the installation of drainage, kerbing, paving and tarmac laying.
- Further experience operating various specialist equipment including gully machines, rough terrain forklifts, rollers, dumpers and small plant.
- An effective team player capable of showing individual initiative, demonstrating a keen eye for detail and the ability to effectively prioritise workloads.
- Ideally seeking a 'Hands on' position where above skills and experiences could be drawn upon and utilised.

- A highly experienced 'Time served' Electrical Technician with extensive knowledge of Health & Safety protocols.
- Responsible for carrying out Health & Safety assessments, inspecting and evaluating reports, liaising with official bodies and members of the public, fire warden training and the testing of electrical appliances.
- Further experience working with the BBC on the installation of studio lighting equipment, testing, fault finding, evaluating and developing new lighting techniques.
- Used to working in environments where initiative, logic and a keen eye for detail are prime requisites, demonstrating excellent communication and customer care skills along with the ability to effectively prioritise workloads.
- Ideally seeking a position where Health & Safety experience and knowledge could be drawn upon and utilised.

AMANDA HUUGET

47 Chessel Drive
Bournemouth, Dorset BH22 1PP
Tel: 01202 888888

SKILLS PROFILE

- An enthusiastic and caring individual having gained qualifications in childcare and animal welfare.
- Recent experience gained as a playworker with Princess Playclubs with responsibility for the monitoring and supervision of children aged five to eleven.
- Liaising with parents and co-workers, organising activities and ensuring rigid adherence to Health & Safety/Health & Hygiene protocols.
- Able to work as part of a team with the ability to demonstrate individual initiative, always ready to offer assistance and eager to learn new methods and techniques.
- Ideally seeking a position within childcare where additional training would be offered to further expand skills base.

WORK PLACEMENT

Playworker (four weeks)

Princess Playgroups, Parkstone, Dorset.

EDUCATION

Darwin School, Wimborne, Dorset
Educated to GCSE standards including Maths and English

Bournemouth and Poole College
City & Guilds – Childcare Certificate

First Aid Childcare Certificate

NVQ level 1 – Animal Welfare

LEISURE INTERESTS

Enjoy playing rounders and netball (member of local team). Swimming, listening to music, especially 'Pop' and doing word-search puzzles.

References Available upon Request

BARRY MORRIS
29 Border Drive
Christchurch, Dorset BH24 3AW
Tel: 01202 444444

SKILLS PROFILE

- More than fifteen years experience of care work within the community.
- Responsible for the safety and welfare of the elderly and infirm, assisting with daily bathing, feeding, dressing, shopping etc.
- Further experiences include dispensing medication, liaising with medical staff, social workers and relevant authorities. Carrying out all duties as required.
- Well-proven communication and customer care skills, able to effectively prioritise workloads with a high level of commitment.
- Seeking a position within the care sector where above skills and experience could be drawn upon and further expanded.

CAREER SUMMARY

In addition to care work, further experiences working on a variety of projects in both the voluntary and commercial sectors, including the "Open Space Conservation Project" as a research assistant. Duties included patrolling, surveying earthworks, leisure and botanical surveys, interviewing residents, report compilations and the maintenance of various equipment.

EDUCATION

Chute Comprehensive School, Verwood, Dorset

Educated to GCE Standards including Maths and English.

QUALIFICATIONS AND ADDITIONAL TRAINING EXPERIENCE

Communication Techniques – Customer Care – Public Relations
Cash Handling and Banking Procedures
Multi-drop Driving
Voluntary work as a countryside warden.
Help for the elderly training scheme. Setting up self help groups for persons suffering from anxiety attacks and phobias.

LEISURE INTERESTS

A keen interest in local history and transport. Visiting car boot sales. Long walks along the seafront and through the New Forest, looking at wildlife. Chairing local self help group with membership of other organisations.

ADDITIONAL INFORMATION

Clean Current Driving Licence

References Available upon Request

WENDY SILVER
107 Wimbledon Road
Bournemouth BH24 8BB
Tel: 01202 000000
E-mail: wendy.silver@yahoo.co.uk

SKILLS PROFILE

- A well educated (Degree level) professional with a wealth of 'front line' customer facing experience.
- Responsible for the planning, development and implementation of a wide range of student programmes, offering support and guidance to young persons who are disadvantaged or in crisis.
- Further experiences include all aspects of administration, report compilation, correspondence and data controls.
- Used to working within demanding environments where initiative, logic and the ability to effectively prioritise are prime requisites.
- Seeking a position where advocacy skills and experiences could be drawn upon and further expanded.

EMPLOYMENT HISTORY

2003-Present   **Information and Advice Worker (Voluntary).**
The Drop-in, Branksome, Dorset.
Providing information, advice, support and a range of interventions for young persons (12-21 years) who are disadvantaged or in crisis, including a health clinic, counselling, advocacy and group work.

1997-2003   **English Teacher (TEFL).**
Working on a wide range of medium term teaching contracts both internationally and within the UK including:

2002-2003	ATM College, Bournemouth, Dorset.
2001-2002	Marton Language College, Bournemouth, Dorset.
1999-2001	Angle Centre, Toledo, Spain.
1998-1999	English Academia de Ingles, Murcia, Spain.
1999	International Study Programmes, Cheltenham, Gloucester.
1997-1998	Moravia Institute, Dehra Dun, India. (Voluntary).

1996-1997   **Delicatessen Assistant.**
Safeway Stores, Muswell Hill, London.
Carrying out all counter service duties within a busy supermarket environment, liaising with customers, organising rotas and stock management

1995-1996   **Co-manager of Alpaca and Llama Farm.**
Province of Canar, Ecuador.
Responsible for assisting with the day to day running including the purchase of medicines, food and hardware, cash handling and bookkeeping, liaising with local farm workers and administering medication to the animals.

CAREER SUMMARY

Additional experience would include working within the voluntary sector as a steward for Oxfam at the Glastonbury Festival and assisting elderly people via the Social Services Committee, Sparking High School.

ACHIEVEMENTS AND ADDITIONAL TRAINING EXPERIENCE

BA (Hons) 2:2 – Social Studies
Newcastle University including six month ERASMUS exchange with Messina University, Sicily.

RSA Cambridge Certificate Teaching English as a Foreign Language
British Language Centre, Madrid, Spain.

Paralegal ILEX Vocational Certificate (level 2)

European Computer Driving Licence (ECDL)

RSA Keyboarding Course

Information & Advice Service Volunteer Training Programme

LEISURE INTERESTS

A keen interest in outdoor activities, especially mountain biking, scuba diving and walking in the mountains. Enjoy painting and sketching using water colour and pastels.

References Available upon Request

FERDINAND OLSEN
412 Castlegate Road
Westhill
Bournemouth BH11 9SS
Tel: 02222 6161999

SKILLS PROFILE

- **A highly regarded technical designer with architectural, interior, refurbishment and fit-out experience.**
- **Responsible for design package development including pharmaceutical research facilities, a wide range of commercial and high-spec residential projects.**
- **Further experiences include management and supervision of staff, sales and purchasing, costing and estimating, negotiating, team building and quality controls.**
- **Reactive to change, proactive to challenge and performance driven.**
- **Ideally seeking a position where vast range of skills and experiences could be drawn upon within a forward thinking company.**

EMPLOYMENT HISTORY

2006   **Technical Co-ordinator (High-rise luxury apartments)**
St Peters Homes, North West London.
Reporting to design manager. Site and head office assignments supervising document control. Analysis and comment of consultant design. Providing advice on procurement issues and products. Resolution of technical issues and management of TQ system for residential developments, from brief development/concept stages through shell and core stage for Seacon and Hornsey sites.

2005   **Cad Technician (Luxury home extensions)**
Glasshouse Conservatories, London.
Product development and design detailing of hardwood timber frame for the bespoke traditional style conservatory manufacturer. Undertaking site investigations and surveys with client liaison. Set-up of Cad based drawing system and component drawing database on AutoCAD LT 97.

2004   **Architectural Technician**
TPS Consultant, Essex.
Design development of entrance cores with toilet and staff change facilities for multiplex business centre in Essex, utilising AutoCAD 2000i.

2003   **Site Architectural Co-ordinator**
Delectable Designs, Bromley, Kent.
Reporting to design team leader. Responsible for overseeing final stages of the construction and fit-out, including fire and smoke control strategy within the £150m project, comprising; pharmaceutical research laboratory buildings, remote plant room and service facilities complex. Troubleshooting construction management and contractor design issues for building envelope, fit-out and landscaping.

CAREER SUMMARY

Agency/contract assignments with architects and designers, performed in the city and central London area.

SIS UK Limited.
Technical advice and operations administration for property maintenance and refurbishment contractor. Projects: Sutton Civic Centre and LTX Corporation (Europe) Limited, Worksop.

Nova Interiors City Limited.
Supervise the implementation design concept for 9 level office fit-out. Co-ordinate the activities of 3 site managers with suppliers and engineering services.

Willis Clayden Connell.
Managed the development and co-ordination of assigned construction packages for the fit-out lead consultant. Project: City European Headquarters, Westminster.

BSP Devenshire Thompson.
Prepare space plan layouts and technical documents for various commercial refurbishment projects.

EDUCATION

St. Anne's School, Wimborne, Dorset

CSE in ten subjects including English and Art

ACHIEVEMENTS AND ADDITIONAL TRAINING EXPERIENCE

City & Guilds – Construction Technician

Timber Engineering and BS 5268 T.R.A.D.A. sponsored course

City & Guilds 2301 – CAD Engineering AutoCAD 2000

Queens Award for Export (team that achieved)

LEISURE INTERESTS

A keen interest in architecture and graphic design. Visiting historical places of interest. Enjoy cycling and running to keep fit.

ADDITIONAL INFORMATION

Clean Current Driving Licence

References Available upon Request

NICHOLAS MARTIN

21 Sycamore Road,
Parkstone, Poole, Dorset BH21 6SL
Tel: 0122222 7881111

SKILLS PROFILE

- An experienced ACOPS registered 'Time served' plumbing and heating engineer.
- Responsible for the installation and maintenance of heating systems, servicing, testing appliances and carrying out refurbishment's.
- Further experience includes the installation and maintenance of all types of plumbing and drainage systems.
- An effective team player capable of demonstrating individual initiative with the ability to effectively prioritise workloads.
- Ideally seeking a position where experience of boiler maintenance and servicing could be drawn upon and utilised.

EMPLOYMENT HISTORY

2000-2006   **Heating Engineer**
James & Sons, Bournemouth, Dorset.
Domestic gas heating maintenance, servicing and testing appliances, refurbishing and installing systems and all aspects of plumbing.

1995-2000   **Plumbing and Heating Engineer**
Self-employed, Bournemouth, Dorset.
Liaising with customers, pricing work, carrying out the installation and maintenance of plumbing and drainage systems.

1991-1995   **Apprentice Plumber**
C.I.T.B. YTS, Salisbury College, Salisbury, Wiltshire.
Training on site and block release at college in plumbing, pipefitting, lead work and other related trades to City & Guilds level.

EDUCATION

Wimborne Technical High School, Wimborne, Dorset.
GCSE Maths and English - CSE in nine subjects

ACHIEVEMENTS AND ADDITIONAL TRAINING EXPERIENCE

City & Guilds Level 11 in Plumbing
ACOPS
In-House Training:
Communication Techniques – Customer Care – Customer Services – Stock Control
Basic Bookkeeping – Cash Handling – Banking Procedures – Quality Controls

LEISURE INTERESTS

Surfing, playing volleyball, member of local gymnasium, going for long countryside walks for relaxation, listening to music, watching films and reading science fiction books.

Current Clean Driving Licence

ROGER CLARKSON
7 Whitehorse Lane
Bournemouth BH8 9AP
Tel: 011120 8179222

SKILLS PROFILE

- A highly regarded (Time served) electronics engineer with extensive international contract management experience.
- Responsible for overseeing the entire installation of a £50m airport construction project from conception through completion.
- Commercially astute with a proven track record of achieving and surpassing targets, working to exacting schedules within high pressure environments, effectively prioritising workloads demonstrating both initiative and logic.
- Ideally seeking a position where vast range of skills, knowledge and experience could be drawn upon and utilised.

EMPLOYMENT HISTORY

2004-2006 **Assistant Manager.**
Fairview Stables, Neath, South Wales.
Responsible for the management of a stud farm, taking care of horses, grounds, tack, stables, vehicles, construction of new site accommodation and stable blocks.

2003-2003 **Airports Site Surveyor.**
Self Employed, Spain.
Visiting various sites in the western regions of mainland Spain surveying, possible locations for future airports.

1999-2002 **Site Manager.**
Airways ATM (Airports) Limited, Salford, Manchester.
Responsible for the on-site management of a £50m airport construction project. Management of Program site integration, liaising with customers and contractors, attending review meetings, monitoring work progress, ensuring adherence to strict quality standards and budgetary constraints.

1996-1999 **Systems Maintenance Engineer.**
Jackson's Engineering, Texas, USA.
Supervision of technicians in comms, radar, nav-aids, data processing, displays and message switching in the maintenance role of an on-line air traffic control centre.

CAREER SUMMARY

Additional employment history would include a wide range of both national and international projects including Technical Manager (Scientific Equipment Services, USA), Systems Maintenance Engineer (Slovak Corporation, Russia), Production Manager (SLF Electronics, Surrey), Unit Test Supervisor (ENS Medical Ltd, Croydon), Installation Engineer (Maston's Radar Field Services, Bedfordshire) and Field Service Engineer with Axons Survey Systems, Norfolk.

EDUCATION

St. Robert's School, Shaftesbury, Dorset

Educated to 'O' level standard in all core subjects including Maths and English

ACHIEVEMENTS AND ADDITIONAL TRAINING EXPERIENCE

Southampton University, Southampton, Hampshire.

Subjects
Electronic Systems Analysis and Design – Electronic Sub-Systems Analysis and Design
Mathematical Methods – Software Programming (Pascal and 'C') – Software Engineering
Project Management – Business Management – Business Studies –French Language Studies

Royal Air Force Training

Ground radar fitting, repairs, installation, commissioning, maintenance
(A wide variety of fixed and air-transportable primary and secondary radar equipment)

LEISURE INTERESTS

A keen interest in bungee jumping and flying small aircraft. Enjoy reading a wide range of literature, listening to 60's and 70's music and travelling around visiting places of historical interest.

ADDITIONAL INFORMATION

References Available upon Request

MARY ROSEN
17 Bennington Drive
Newport, S. Wales
Tel: 00000 000000
E-mail: maryrosen@ntlworld.com

SKILLS PROFILE

- **A highly experienced Personal Assistant/Secretary with extensive 'front line' customer facing experience.**
- **Responsible for overseeing and co-ordinating projects, producing minutes and monthly statistical analysis, diary management, data controls and security.**
- **Further experiences include organising travel arrangements, conferences and meetings, direct customer liaison, secretarial and administrative support.**
- **Used to working within high-pressure environments, demonstrating well-proven communication skills and the ability to effectively prioritise workloads.**
- **Ideally seeking a position where above skills and experiences could be drawn upon and further expanded.**

EMPLOYMENT HISTORY

1997-2006   **Harmans – Trading as Davis Brothers, Newport, Gwent.**
CTC Systems – Formerly Capstone Engineering.

PA to Managing Director.
Harmans – Trading as Davis Brothers, Newport, Gwent.
Organising conferences, meetings and travel itineraries, producing management meeting minutes, monthly sales analysis and electronic presentations. Assisting MD during the due diligence phase of Harmans acquisition of Davis Bros, managing electronic diary, initiating operation of electronic time sheets and holiday records, implementing system for the protection of proprietary information.

Executive Secretary.
CTC Systems – Formerly Capstone Engineering.
Secretarial support for departmental executive and managers, organising travel for thirty plus engineers, point of contact customer liaison, processing customer fault/observation reports and producing monthly analysis. Time sheet, clock card, expense claim and secondment administration, supervising allocation of lap-top computers and pool cars.

1995-1996   **Community Services Assistant.**
British Blue Cross, Wimbledon, London.
Administrative and secretarial support on all aspects of Blue Cross Community Services, visiting vulnerable clients, deputising for Assistant Branch Director and other branch officers in their absence.

1994-1995   **Sales Administrator.**
Sarsons Brothers, London.
Co-ordinating sales and manufacture of military bespoke uniforms, managing correspondence relating to customer complaints and payment problems, calculating invoices, organising bankers orders and VAT exemption for HM Forces officers.

1993-1994   **Administrator.**
Citizens Advice Bureau, Basingstoke, Hampshire.
Working as a voluntary administrator within a busy citizens advice bureau.

1986-1993   **Sales Administration Manager.**
BELL Chemicals, London.
Responsible for running the sales office of a multi-national company, recruiting, training and supervising sales administrators, organising and leading sales department to successfully achieve ISO9002 accreditation. Liaising between world-wide customers, sales executives, production and shipping departments. Co-ordinating transition of manual sales order entry system onto remote mainframe. Obtaining, recording and allocating foreign currency, reconciling petty cash returns. Organising and supervising relocation of London office to Liverpool.

ACHIEVEMENTS AND ADDITIONAL TRAINING EXPERIENCE

RSA Secretarial Course

Computer Literacy
(MS Windows 2000, Office XP, Word, Excel, PowerPoint, Outlook, Internet, Intranet)

In-House Training
Communication Techniques – Customer Care – Staff Training & Supervision – Recruitment
Stock Controls – Handling Confidential Information – Security Protocols – Data Entry
Diary Management – Quality Controls – Basic Bookkeeping – Health & Safety

LEISURE INTERESTS

Enjoy visiting places of historical interest, listening to a wide range of music, completing crosswords, socialising with friends and family.

References Available upon Request

SIMON GREEN
17 Jupiter Close
Bournemouth BH1 4BB
Tel: 01202 111222   Mob: 07860 222111

SKILLS PROFILE

- More than twenty years experience working within the hospitality sector.
- Responsible for the day to day running of busy establishments, supervising and training staff, stock management and direct customer liaison.
- Further experiences include cash handling, customer services, promotions, displays, advertising, administration and basic bookkeeping.
- Used to working within high-pressure environments where initiative and logic are prime requisites, demonstrating well-proven communication and customer care skills.
- Ideally seeking a position where "People Skills" could be drawn upon and further expanded.

EMPLOYMENT HISTORY

2006   **Assistant Manager.**
The Candy Box, Bournemouth, Dorset.
Responsible for the day-to-day running of a busy retail outlet in the absence of management, liaising with customers, stock controls, cash handling, operating EPOS systems, security protocols and banking.

2002-2005   **Second Steward/Relief Manager.**
Southdown Conservative Club, Southbourne, Dorset.
Carrying out all duties including the supervision and training of up to ten staff, preparing rotas, stock management, cellar duties, customer liaison, security protocols (key holder), bank reconciliation's and basic administration.

2001-2002   **Bar Person.**
Maritime Golf Park, Bournemouth, Dorset.
Similar duties to above including food service and end of day reconciliation's.

1999-2002   **Bar Person/Supervisor.**
Selwyn Hotel, Parkstone, Dorset.
Working within a renowned three star hotel, supervising bar service to private banqueting and party functions, training new staff, food service and stock management.

1992-1999   **Proprietor.**
Phenomenon, Bournemouth, Dorset.
Operating own business for the promotion of psychic and holistic fayres, advertising, organising, planning, booking venues, administration and 1-2-1 client counselling.

1988-1992   **Roofing Engineer.**
Slaters Limited, East End, Derbyshire..
Carrying out all roofing and general maintenance requirements to mobile homes.

EDUCATION

Grange secondary School, Cardiff, South Wales.

Educated to GCE standard in all core subjects including Maths and English

ACHIEVEMENTS AND ADDITIONAL TRAINING EXPERIENCE

City & Guilds – Trainee Chef

In-House Training
Communication Techniques – Customer Care – Customer Services – Cash Handling
Stock Management – Operating EPOS Systems – Security Protocols – Cellar Duties
Basic Administration – Basic Bookkeeping – Staff Training & Supervision - Displays
Promotions – Advertising – Health & Safety – Health & Hygiene

LEISURE INTERESTS

Enjoy keeping fit, swimming and playing tennis. Going for long countryside walks. Reading a wide range of literature, especially psychology profiling. Home computing.

ADDITIONAL INFORMATION

Clean Current Driving Licence

Conversational Spanish, Italian, German and Arabic.

References Available upon Request

GRAHAM GOLD
29 Spur Road
Poole BH29 8TT
Tel: 00000 111111
E-mail: grahamgg@aol.com

SKILLS PROFILE

- A highly motivated individual with extensive 'Hands on' Sound/Lighting experience within the theatre and entertainment industry.
- With a broad portfolio of pantomime and theatre productions, responsibilities have included the supervision of technicians and the overall running of shows.
- Further experiences include working aboard cruise liners and touring with various production companies.
- Used to working within high-pressure environments where both initiative and logic are prime requisites, demonstrating well-proven communication skills and the ability to effectively prioritise.
- Ideally seeking a position where above skills and experiences could be drawn upon and further expanded.

EMPLOYMENT HISTORY

2006 **PNC Theatre Engineer.**
Located in Thornton Hotels in Coss. Resident Thornton Gold Technician at Delafont hotel, Crete.

2005 **Sound System Engineer/Production Manager.**
50 Date tour of the UK as a sound system engineer for Lee Audio with Larry Harper and his sixteen piece swing band tribute to Sinatra, promoted by Grand Music. Sailing Europe and Mediterranean as deputy production manager on P & O Arither.

2004 **Number 1 Sound/Sound Engineer.**
As number 1 sound on Dr. Spock pantomime at the London Hammersmith Apollo for Eden Productions. Sailing the Caribbean as sound engineer on MV Jasmine Flower. Touring with Kallico Indian Dance Company. Sound production work for Lo Audio- Jane Mary and Hoggey Books Tours.

2003 **Number 1 Spot/Sound Engineer.**
10 week tour of 'Rusty, a musical tribute' for Casio Productions, starring Daren Neston and directed by John Blaser. Sailing the Mediterranean as a sound engineer on D3 cruise ship. Summer season as number 1 spot on Jane Carson show at Wembley.

2002 **TV Extra/Technical Manager/Number 1 Sound.**
Working as a TV extra on East Winds with Jason Brown and Dona Kebab. Touring UK as a technical manager with Hales Chinese Dance Company. Number 1 sound on Dr. Spock pantomime at Southampton Westgate for Eden Productions, starring Mike Breeze, Dafney Wilson and Brian Goaty.

2001 **Stage Manager/Lighting & Sound Technician.**
Touring as stage manager with Bounty Ballet Company. Sailing as lighting and sound technician on Seatours MS Moonbeam.

2000 Stage Manager.
Sailing Southern Europe as stage manager on MV Silver Stream. Summer season as stage manager for 'Joseph & the Techni-coloured Dreamcoat' at the Froth Theatre, Isle of Sheppey, for Dick Miles, Sark International Productions. Stage manager for 'Babes in the Wood' Gruff Theatre, Isle of Sheppey.

1999 Sound & Lighting Technician.
Working aboard two ships, MV Costa lot and MV Costa prettypenny, sailing the Caribbean as a lighting and sound technician.

1998 Lighting & Sound Technician.
Summer season at Sidmouth for the 'Fall about laughing Show' with the Rolands, Bernie and Fred Cash. Canderella pantomime with Andy Caps and Rachel Dixon from TV's Home with the Birdies.

EDUCATION

Grange Hill Secondary, Bridport, Dorset.

'O' level in seven subjects including English

CSE in six subjects

LEISURE INTERESTS

Enjoy playing guitar, sea fishing, reading a wide range of literature, visiting the theatre and socialising with friends.

References Available upon Request

DAMIEN CASH

888 Wilburn Avenue
Bridport BR2 56QT
Tel: 00000 111111

SKILLS PROFILE

- A highly experienced technically qualified senior materials engineer.
- Fully conversant with the principles of management for road construction projects in developing countries within both Asia and the Middle East.
- Experienced in asphalt and concrete mix designs and the evaluation of highway construction materials.
- Extensive knowledge of highway construction techniques and laboratory test procedures.
- Ideally seeking a position where above skills and experiences could be drawn upon

---

EMPLOYMENT HISTORY

2001-2006   **Senior Quality Assurance Engineer.**
Matrix International, India..
Responsible for the management of quality control for a 120km rehabilitation project for the Dhaka to Syhlet highway. Formulated a detailed site investigation program, especially in new alignment areas where the road crossed paddi fields. Advised the contractor's on the treatment required in soft ground locations after recommendations had been given by a geotechnical expert. Treatments included removal of weak soils, installation of a geotextile fabric and in deeper locations the use of a composite geotextile membrane to help reinforce the high embankments. Supervising 15 technical staff, overseeing day-to-day site and laboratory operations. Other duties included approval of aggregate and concrete mix designs, advising on technical parameters used to approve asphalt mixes and checking road furniture/markings.

2000-2001   **Senior Quality Assurance Engineer.**
Matrix International, Vietnam.
Responsible for the management of quality control for a 95km rehabilitation project for highway 1A phase 2. Supervision of up to 12 local inspectors. Daily inspection of contract to check construction process, crushing facilities, asphalt and concrete mixing plants.

1999-2000   **Independent Consultant.**
Employed in the U.K as a materials engineer or technician, on short-term contracts in site or permanent laboratories.

1997-1998   **Senior Soils/Materials Engineer.**
Delu International, Vietnam.
Engaged to oversee construction of granular and bituminous materials for phase 2 of highway 5, where the existing road was upgraded to dual carriageway standard. Checking the contractors laboratories including mobilization. Assessment of pavement trials, quarry and existing pavement surveys. Funding: Japanese overseas bank.

1996-1996   **Laboratory Manager.**
                     Matrix Internationl, Japan.
Responsible for the planning, design, establishment and daily operations of a soils laboratory. Modified the Test Procedure, Quality Assurance manuals and established the Calibration manual. Experience gained in quality assurance systems, calibration procedures, computer skills and effective stress testing.

1993-1995   **Student. (York University)**
This specialist degree course was structured around Quarry and Road surface Engineering, Mineral Industries Management, Safety and Environmental issues.

1988-1993   **Senior Materials Engineer.**
Responsible for the setting up and management of on-site materials laboratories. Overseeing day-to day operations including approval of material sources, daily liaison with consultant, assessment of quarries, plant and preparation of reports. In 1991 achieved the first Namas Accreditation for an on-site laboratory facility operating under the Department of Transport contracts.

ACHIEVEMENTS AND ADDITIONAL TRAINING EXPERIENCE

B Eng. - Quarrying and Road surface Engineering

HNC Civil Engineering

C & G Concrete Technology

DAPS Asphalt Technology

NATA Quality Management in the Laboratory

PROFESSIONAL MEMBERSHIPS

Member of the Asphalt Institute (I.A.T)

Graduate member of the Institute of Civil Engineers

LEISURE INTEREST

A keen interest in cricket, Chelsea football club, Poole speedway, gardening, stocks and shares, home computing, socialising with friends and family.

ADDITIONAL INFORMATION

Clean Current Driving License

References Available upon Request

TANIA TURNER
12 Marine Drive
Bournemouth BH29 2TT
Tel: 11111 111111   Mob: 00000 000000

PROFILE

An enthusiastic individual seeking to pursue and develop a career within office administration and prepared to undertake any additional training toward this goal. Currently studying to gain computer literacy and information technology qualification.

EMPLOYMENT HISTORY

2005-2006   **Career Development.**
Time out from full-time employment to pursue adult education course to gain computer qualifications and update skills base.

1997-2005   **Cleaner.**
Sallys Property Services, Poole, Dorset.
Carrying out general cleaning duties within both school and office environments, using hazardous cleaning chemicals, operating buffers and other specialised equipment.

CAREER SUMMARY

Priori to a career break to raise a family, additional work experience would include working as an entertainer with Butlins, visiting holiday camps throughout the southern region with a troupe of Jugglers.

EDUCATION

St. Joseph Secondary School, Poole, Dorset.
Educated to GCSE standard in all core subjects including Maths and English

ACHIEVEMENTS AND ADDITIONAL TRAINING EXPERIENCE

Computer Literacy and Information Technology (CLAIT)

In-House Training
Communication Techniques – Customer Care – Cash Handling – Operating Tills
Security Protocols – Operating Specialist Machinery & Equipment – Production Procedures
Health & Safety – Health & Hygiene

LEISURE INTERESTS

Enjoy keeping fit, member of local fitness club, swimming, dog walking and exploring the countryside. Reading a wide range of literature, listening to all types of music and socialising with friends.

References Available upon Request

MALCOLM DAVIES
24 The Birches
Ringwood BH25 4GH
Tel: 00990 222333

SKILLS PROFILE

- An enthusiastic individual seeking to develop a technical career within the entertainment industry.
- A keen interest in all aspects of production including sound, lighting, studio techniques and music.
- Previous experience of electronic engineering, laboratory technician and software development.
- Eager to take advantage of any training opportunity within the entertainment sector to further career goal.

CAREER SUMMARY

Software Development Engineer. EPS, London W1.
Software development of real-time laser control system firmware. Program/test harness design and coding (in C).

Laboratory Technician, Poole College of Further Education, Dorset.
Assisting lecturers and students in practical workshops, constructing and maintaining demonstration apparatus. Using a wide range of equipment and machine tools including lathes, welding gear and computers.

Trainee Electronics Engineer, Wimborne Tecnologies, Dorset.
Producing schematic circuit diagrams from prototype boards, testing and validating specifications.

EDUCATION, ACHIEVEMENTS AND ADDITIONAL TRAINING EXPERIENCE

ONC Electrical Engineering

City & Guilds TT3

Access to Health & Science
(Anatomy & Physiology – Biochemistry)

Tinternell Secondary School, Christchurch, Dorset
GCE in seven subjects including Maths and English

LEISURE INTERESTS

Enjoy computer programming, music composition and recording, having developed a number of small business web sites (also familiar with the use of sequencers, SMPTE and multitrack recording techniques). A keen interest in ecology and permaculture (especially renewable energy technologies), herbalism and aromatherapy.

References Available upon Request

56

PAULA JACKSON
222 Green Road
Wimborne WM5 4TR
Tel: 01111 222444   Mob: 01111 222333

SKILLS PROFILE

- **An enthusiastic individual seeking a return to employment, after having taken a career break to raise a family and update skills.**
- **Responsibilities have included the day-to-day management of a club bar, supervision of staff, cash handling, banking, operating EPOS systems, cellar duties, stock management and direct customer liaison.**
- **Further customer facing experience within the hotel and catering industry.**
- **An effective team player capable of using individual initiative, demonstrating well-proven communication and customer care skills along with the ability to effectively prioritise.**
- **Ideally seeking to develop skills and experience within an administrative or receptionist position whilst keen to participate in any further training toward this goal.**

EMPLOYMENT HISTORY

2004-2006   **Career Break/Further Education.**
Time out from full-time employment to raise a family whilst undertaking Information Technology and skills update courses.

2002-2994   **Bar Person.**
Pot Black Snooker Club, Wimborne, Dorset.
Responsible for the day-to-day management of a busy snooker club bar, including staff training and supervision, stock controls, cash handling, cellar duties, banking and security.

2000-2001   **Waitress.**
Faulty Towers, Bournemouth, Dorset.
Working as a waitress in a small privately owned hotel catering for twenty guests, assisting with the preparation of food, setting up and serving.

CAREER SUMMARY

Additional experience working in a variety of roles on short to medium term agency contracts, including front of house hotel duties, table service in various restaurants and fast food outlets. Liaising with customers, taking orders, preparing food, cash handling, operating EPOS tills, maintaining strict Health & Safety/Health & Hygiene protocols.

ACHIEVEMENTS AND ADDITIONAL TRAINING EXPERIENCE

Computer Literacy and Information Technology (CLAIT)

In-House Training
Communication Techniques – Customer Care – Customer Services – Cash Handling
Operating EPOS Systems – Staff Supervision & Training – Banking Procedures
Security Protocols (Key Holder) – Stock Management – Cellar Duties – Food Preparation
Health & Safety – Health & Hygiene

EDUCATION

Muddleswich High School, Manchester, Lancashire.

GCSE in five subjects including Maths and English

LEISURE INTERESTS

A keen swimmer, visiting places of interest, reading a wide range of literature, socialising with friends and family.

References Available upon Request

SARAH GATES

2A Beach Road
Bournemouth BH19 9GH
Tel: 01202 111222

SKILLS PROFILE

- A highly motivated enthusiastic individual with extensive care and retail experience.
- Responsible for the day to day welfare of mentally ill persons, administering medication, preparing meals, report writing, attending meetings and monitoring individual progress.
- Further experience of direct customer liaison, cash handling, operating EPOS systems, stock management, banking procedures and security protocols.
- Used to working within high-pressure environments demonstrating excellent communication and customer care skills along with the ability to effectively prioritise.
- Ideally seeking to draw upon above skills and experiences to develop a career within the probation or prison services, whilst keen to undertake training toward this goal.

EMPLOYMENT HISTORY

2003-2006   **Support Worker.**
Prama Sheltered Lodgings, Bournemouth, Dorset.
Assisting with the day to day needs and requirements of mentally ill persons within a sheltered communal environment.

2000-2003   **Sales Advisor.**
Cotton Fayre, Bournemouth, Dorset.
Working in a busy retail outlet advising and assisting customers, cash handling, operating EPOS tills, stock management, security protocols and banking.

1998-2000   **Support Worker.**
Prama Sheltered Lodgings, Bournemouth, Dorset.
As above including cooking and administering medication, attending meetings offering progress reports and monitoring responses.

CAREEER SUMMARY

Additional experience includes working as a retail shop assistant with 'Timothy Value,' photo processing and chamber maid.

ACHIEVEMENTS AND ADDITIONAL TRAINING EXPERIENCE

In-House Training

Communication Techniques – Customer Care – Customer Services – Stock Management
Cash Handling – Operating EPOS Systems – Promotions – Displays – Security Protocols
Team Building – Stress Management – Handling Confidential Information
Basic Administration – Health & Hygiene – Health & Safety

EDUCATION

Southhall Secondary School, Bournemouth, Dorset.

Educated to GCSE standard in all core subjects including Maths and English.

LEISURE INTERESTS

Enjoy keeping fit, cycling, playing badminton and cross country hiking. Reading a wide range of literature and socialising with friends.

References Available upon Request

MICHAEL BOARDEN
2 Hook Road
Bournemouth BH6 6FG
Tel: 01202 333333

SKILLS PROFILE

- A fully qualified 'Time Served' mechanical engineer.
- Responsible for the day to day running of a busy production environment including quality controls (ISO 9002), stock controls and man-management.
- Further experience operating a wide range of lathes and milling machines including CNC.
- Used to working within high-pressure environments where both initiative and logic are prime requisites, demonstrating first class communication and customer care skills.
- Ideally seeking a position where above skills and experiences could be drawn upon and utilised.

EMPLOYMENT HISTORY

1989-2006   **Machinist/Inspector.**
Lazeby Engineering, Christchurch, Dorset.
Responsible for the operation of a wide range of lathes and milling machines including CNC. Attaining promotion to chief inspector, managing the day to day running of the entire workshop including staff management and training, quality controls (ISO 9002) stock controls and shipping.

CAREER SUMMARY

Further experience working in a self-employed role carrying out a wide range of engineering contracts.

EDUCATION

Ruperts Secondary School, Nottingham.
Educated to GCE standard in all core subjects including Maths and English.

ACHIEVEMENTS AND ADDITIONAL TRAINING EXPERIENCE

City & Guilds T1, T2, T3, T4 – Engineering

In-House Training
Communication Techniques – Customer Care – Customer Services – Stock Management
Quality Controls (ISO 9002) – Administrative Procedures – Security Protocols
Team Building – Health & Safety

LEISURE INTERESTS

Enjoy playing golf (handicap of eighteen), watching and occasionally participating in cricket matches. Member of Royal British Legion and local Conservative Club.

References Available upon Request

CHRISTOPHER ROBINS
123 Grassy Way
Bournemouth, Dorset BH11 3KK
Tel: 012222 8811009   Mob: 00001 00011
E-mail: christopherrobins@hotmail.com

SKILLS PROFILE

- Experienced IT manager, both technically and commercially qualified, fully conversant with the principals of project management, business analysis and networking.
- Responsible for the day-to-day running of configuration room, supervision and training of (25+) staff to ISO standards.
- Working closely in partnership with customers delivering targeted, cost effective systems and solutions.
- Excellent communication skills, a logical mind and the ability to develop and implement technical procedures.
- Seeking a position where IT Technical/Systems Engineering skills of installations, maintenance, administration and design could be drawn upon.

IT SKILLS SUMMARY

Microsoft Certified, Windows 2000/NT4/98/95/3.1 Office 97/2000, Project 98/2000, SQL 7/2000, Lotus Notes, Outlook & Exchange 5.5, ILS, LANS/WANS, Proxy Server, Firewalls, Web Design, Server & Desktop Builds, Microsoft NT4 Workstation/Server (MCP).

CAREER HISTORY

2001-Present **Team Leader Installation Engineer.**
Alpha Computer Systems.
Working on the Willow's Refresh project. Overseeing the installation of checkouts and customer service areas and Network. De-installing and re-installing all computer EPOS equipment at Mantrax and Superstores nation-wide and rebuilding as necessary. Working on Willow's Home Shopping (Internet based) System moves, repairs and upgrades. Liaising closely with system support to ensure that any impact on trading is kept to a minimum.

2000-2001 **Engineering & IT Manager.**
Alpha Computer Systems.
Responsible for managing the day to day operation of the configuration room, overseeing eight contract engineers, staff training, scheduling, administering and supporting the internal IT system and network, ensuring maintenance of the vehicle fleet. Ensuring that the agreed schedule of rollout was maintained liaising with project/key client-side managers and staff. Discussed and implemented improvements, attending regular meetings. Team responsibility for the configuration, testing and installation of 31 pieces of equipment for each of the forty new Tresco's Tiger sites (Tresco/Bell Alliance).

1999-2000 **Senior Systems Engineer.**
PLB Solutions Limited.
Providing small-scale network and computer installations for SME's, carrying out detailed analysis and planning, liaising with clients, producing detailed costing and assessment reports, building, configuring and installing.

1999-1999	**Systems Engineer.**
	Churchfield IT.
	Contracted on a rollout for Tresco's involving server hardware and software upgrades at several hundred superstore sites.

1997-1999	**Systems Engineer.**
	Land Mail.
	Part of the Land Mail team assisting with the implementation of the new C.A.A. (in-house) coding system, testing and running system trials.

1995-1996	**Property Developer Landlord.**
	Self-employed.
	Converting business property into sub-units to let.

1988-1995	**Shop Proprietor.**
	Self-employed.
	Responsible for the complete day to day running and management of a town centre shop offering dry cleaning and associated services.

1985-1988	**Senior Research Analyst.**
	Barclaycard.
	Working as a team leader within the International Cashiers Department, investigating accounting errors in all European currencies.

EDUCATION

Gladstone Comprehensive School, Gwent, South Wales.
3 'A' levels, 4 'O' levels, 7 CSE's.

Brighton Technical College, Brighton, East Sussex
Business Studies Diploma – Pass with credits.

LEISURE INTERESTS

A keen interest in amateur dramatics having performed in several productions including "Ali Barbar and The Forty Theives." Cycling, travel, camping, computers and electronics.

ADDITIONAL INFORMATION

Car Owner with Clean Current Driving Licence

References Available upon Request.

PETER SIMMONS
22 Chalk Road,
Bournemouth, Dorset BH10 6SA
Tel: 017171 5444497

SKILLS PROFILE

- An experienced, qualified electrician with specialist knowledge of the control of air conditioning and refrigeration units.
- Responsible for the management and supervision of (25+) staff, carrying out on-site work throughout the United Kingdom, installing bespoke refrigeration systems.
- Carrying out repairs, refurbishment's, trouble shooting, liaising with clients, stock management, security, report writing and general administration.
- Used to working within high-pressure environments where initiative and logic are prime requisites. Able to effectively prioritise with a keen eye for detail.
- Ideally seeking a position where above skills and experience of refrigeration control systems would be drawn upon and utilised.

EMPLOYMENT HISTORY

2002-2006 **Electrician.**
Self-employed, Bournemouth, Dorset.
Carrying out electrical repairs and general property maintenance for private sector clients.

1999-2002 **Supervisor/Labourer.**
B.T.S. Recruitment Ltd. Poole, Dorset.
Working with and organising a team of men whose duties were preparing fuel cans for the British Forces working within the 'Parkstone' fuel depot.

1991-1999 **Senior Electrician.**
Jackson's Food Display Systems Ltd, Bournemouth, Dorset.
Design and build of refrigerated display cabinets. Duties included the repair and refurbishment of on-site cabinets, fault finding and all aspects of the factory maintenance. Travelling to locations throughout the United Kingdom.

1980-1991 **Security Technician.**
Self-employed, Bournemouth, Dorset.
Working on various contracts within the United Kingdom, Europe and Nicaragua including British Aerospace. Duties included inspection of armaments for the Tornado and Strike Master projects.

EDUCATION

Purbeck Boys School, Wareham, Dorset.

11 CSE's including Maths and English

Poole and Bournemouth College, Bournemouth, Dorset.

City & Guilds 235/B Electrician

Peter Simmons CV Cont……

ACHIEVEMENTS AND ADDITIONAL TRAINING EXPERIENCE

<u>In-House Training</u>

Communication Techniques
Customer Care
Stock Management
Security Procedures
Management and Administration
Health & Safety
Fire Prevention

LEISURE INTERESTS

A keen interest in golf. Playing five-a-side football at local leisure centre. Cookery and gardening.

ADDITIONAL INFORMATION

Clean Current Driving Licence

References Available Upon Request.

RICHARD PARSONS
55 Highhill Road
Bournemouth, Dorset BH6 3NN
Tel: 01222 42222111

SKILLS PROFILE

- A highly motivated professional with more than fifteen years management experience within the hospitality sector.
- Responsible for the day to day running of busy hotels and public houses, staff supervision and training, customer service, liaising with guests, cash handling, banking and security.
- Further experiences have included stock management, cellar duties, promotions, advertising, event organising, trouble-shooting, maintaining rigid health and hygiene guidelines.
- Used to working within high-pressure environments demonstrating the ability to effectively prioritise with a keen eye for detail. Well proven management, communication and customer care skills.
- Ideally seeking a position where above skills and experience could be drawn upon and further expanded.

EMPLOYMENT HISTORY

1999-2006 **Duty Manager.**
The Woodcutter Inn, Burley, Hampshire.
Responsible for the day-to-day running of busy public house including staff supervision and training, stock management, customer services, cash handling and banking.

1992-1999 **Manager.**
The Jug of Ale, Salisbury, Wiltshire.
Duties as above.

1988-1992 **Manager**
The Sunrise Hotel, Stow-on-the-wold, Gloucestershire.

1986-1988 **Manager**
The Fox and Hounds, Lacock, Wiltshire.

ACHIEVEMENTS & ADDITIONAL TRAINING EXPERIENCE

Communication Techniques – Customer Care – Stock Controls – Customer Services
Management & Staff Training – Cash Handling & Banking Procedures
Health & Safety – Health & Hygiene

LEISURE INTERESTS

Enjoy playing pool and darts.
Cooking (Chinese and traditional dishes)

References Available upon Request

JOHN BRIDE
Flat 125
Cranleigh Road
Reading, Berkshire
Tel: 00000 000000

SKILLS PROFILE

- A highly motivated individual with more than twenty years experience working within the construction, ventilation and stores industries.
- Responsible for working on a wide range of construction projects, building reservoirs, laying pipes, wet and dry concrete finishing, installing cladding and ducting.
- Further experiences include staff supervision (25 persons), allocation of contracts, preparation of time sheets, reading blueprints, liaising with architects, designers and relevant site personnel.
- Used to working within high-pressure environments where initiative and logic are prime requisites, demonstrating excellent communication and customer care skills along with the ability to effectively prioritise workloads.
- Ideally seeking a position, preferably in a general maintenance or similar role, where wide range of skills and experiences could be drawn upon and utilised.

CAREER SUMMARY

Working on a wide range of medium term contracts in a sub contracted role for various recruitment agencies including Sam Johnson Services of Swindon, building reservoirs, laying pipes, wet and dry concrete finishing. Additional work at the Worth Air Base installing cladding for hangers, laying pipes for drainage and building utilities. Working as an erector for Can-O-Ducts, Reading, installing ducting for air conditioning units within offices, factory units and large shopping complexes. Liaising with architects and site personnel, reading blueprints, following rigid Health & Safety guidelines. Further experience include working as a storeman with Ford Motor Company, commencing as a parts stacker within the shipping department and progressing to storeman/checker with responsibility for stock management. Ensuring parts were delivered to exacting time schedules, liaising with department heads and senior management.

EDUCATION, ACHIEVEMENTS AND ADDITIONAL TRAINING EXPERIENCE

In-House Training
Communication Techniques – Customer Care – Stock Management – Team Building
Warehouse Procedures – Quality Controls – Time Management – Security Protocols
Basic Administration – Use of Specialist Tools & Equipment – Health & Safety

Educate to GCE 'O' level standards in all core subjects including Maths and English

LEISURE INTERESTS

Enjoy painting (Designed and painted winning carnival float based on the Jungle Book theme for the Reading Carnival). Going for long walks, socialising with friends, watching football and golf.

References Available upon Request

ANDREW MELBOURNE
229 Cavendish Avenue
Bournemouth, Dorset BH17 1ZX
Tel: 01111 111111   Mob: 00000 000000
E-mail: andrew_melbou@aol.com

SKILLS PROFILE

- An experienced IT manager, technically and commercially qualified, fully conversant with the principles of project management, business analysis and networking.
- Responsible for developing and deploying IT strategies, managing multiple projects such as LAN/WAN rollout across multiple sites, controlling budgets, negotiating contracts and administering the IT department including purchasing and recruitment.
- Further responsibilities included board presentations, generating cost v benefit v risk analysis, developing financial and technical projections, leading in-house seminars and writing functional specifications mainly within SME's in the private sector.
- An effective presenter, self-motivated with proven business, team management, customer facing and leadership skills. Ideally placed for a senior appointment within commercial IT/project management and willing to commute or relocate.

IT SKILLS SUMMARY

OPERATING SYSTEMS	Win 3.X, Win 9.X, Win NT, Win XP, Win ME, Novell Netware to version 5.DOS, Frame Relay, TCP/IP, Hubs, Routers, MUX, Cabling Technologies, IBM 3270, Telephone Switches-Ericsson, SDX/Lucent
APPLICATIONS	MS Office Suite, various related databases (MS Access, Dbase, Paradox, FoxPro, Omnis, Filemaker), Lotus 123, Harvard Graphics, PowerPoint, MS Publisher, MS Project, Languages (Basic, Cobol, Fortran).
HARDWARE	WAN, LAN, TCP, IP, MUX, IBM PC, Apple Computers, IBM 3174/3274,

EMPLOYMENT HISTORY

2005-2006 Consultant/PA.
Martin Bradshaw Limited, Tadley, Hampshire..
Implementing an enhanced IT communications system within a busy legal practice. Restructuring the office administration within the immigration side including case preparations, work loads, booking procedures and recruitment.

1997-2005 Group IT Manager. (2 Companies).
Medusa Enterprises/Excalibur Games, Basingstoke.
Responsible for the global communications including LAN/WAN infrastructures at head office and four remote sites (2 overseas), developing new systems and procedures, liaising with directors and senior management, coordinating and streamlining operations, purchasing equipment, software and third party services, negotiating contracts and service agreements, maintaining operating costs within budgetary constraints, management and supervision of staff.

1991-1996 Information Centre Coordinator/Project Manager.
Broadhurst International, Tadley, Hampshire.
Supporting installed software/hardware at two UK sites, reviewing and developing new systems, staff training, communication links (leased line, ISDN, 3174 etc.)

CAREER SUMMARY 1980-1985

Support Manager - Sun Valley Computer Centre, Tadley.
Engineering Manager – (PC & Peripherals) FMG Ltd, Basingstoke, Hampshire.
Programmer - Goldrush Computer Systems Ltd, Basingstoke, Hampshire.
Sales - (PC Systems) Sun Valley Computer Centre, Tadley.

QUALIFICATIONS, ACHIEVEMENTS & ADDITIONAL TRAINING EXPERIENCE

Currently studying Webmaster (incorporating Oxford, Cambridge & RSA Global Communications.
City & Guilds OOP with Java level 3, Association of Computer Professionals Initial Award

Novell Netware 5 – Certified Netware Administrator
Ericsson BP250 Engineering & Programming (PBX Telephone Switch)
Scheiddeger Bookkeeping Diploma (Distinction)
Apple Computers – Engineering
IBM – Marketing

WAN – Design and implementation of Frame Relay Network to carry voice, data, e-mail, intranet and internet services.
Telecommunications – Reduction of approximately 20% in all call costs (£20,000) 1997-2000
IT Department – Creation and development of two IT departments (1997-2000)
Flight Booking System – Implementation and staff training (1997)

LEISURE INTERESTS

A keen interest in golf and angling, teaching course fishing to youngsters. Entertaining at home, visiting friends and reading fiction for relaxation.

ADDITIONAL INFORMATION

Clean Current Driving Licence

References Available upon Request

HARRY JAMES
14 Airway Road,
Bournemouth BH17 1WA
Tel: 01234 123456

SKILLS PROFILE

- Recent experience as an **Employment Advisor** with particular interest in **Self-employment strategies.**
- Skills include identifying employment barriers and providing solutions towards career direction and development.
- Responsibilities have included management and supervision of staff, training and overall security for property and personal data.
- Computer literate, able to work in high-pressure environments where initiative and logic are essential tools. Highly motivated, methodical, paying great attention to detail.
- Well placed to continue developing career, undertaking further training to enhance skills base.

ACHIEVEMENTS

Re-designed impeller for water-cooling inboard/outboard engines (Tellycraft U.S.A.)
Invented and patented "Quick change electrical plug," (Shown on Tomorrows World.)
Re-designed lubrication system and carried out conversions to Skoda cars.
Invented vehicle security device, capable of interfacing with all other systems.

WORK HISTORY

1999-2006   **Senior Careers Tutor.**
ABC Training Services, Bournemouth.
Instructing classes of unemployed people, showing them how to prepare CV's, fill-out application forms, interview/telephone techniques and how to carry out an effective job-search etc.

1998-1999   **Inventor/Designer.**
Self-Employed, Bournemouth.
Inventing, designing and patenting vehicle security device. Carrying out extensive research and investigating market responses prior to production.

1994-1998   **Maintenance Engineer.**
Self-Employed, Bournemouth.
Carrying out old property renovations, refurbishments and conversions. Installation of suspended ceilings, plumbing, painting, decorating and new build.

1989-1994   **Maintenance Manager.**
PDQ, Bournemouth.
Responsible for complete upkeep of hotel (100 + rooms) and all facilities, i.e. Offices, gymnasium, nursery etc. Purchasing of equipment, new build and refurbishment. Electrical, plumbing, heating, decorating and security.

1985-1989   **Vehicle Technician.**
A & B Mobile Services, Bournemouth.
Operating recovery service, attending breakdowns, servicing, overhauls, conversions and restoration of vehicles. High performance engine rebuilds and modifications.

TRAINING AND QUALIFICATIONS

Motor Vehicle Technician - City and Guilds – Part 1
Motor Vehicle Technician - City and Guilds – Part 11

Fire Prevention/Practical - Dorset Fire Service Certification.

EDUCATION

Charles Ingram Secondary School, Basingstoke, Hampshire

GCE in eight subjects including Maths and English

LEISURE INTERESTS

Historical research/Archaeology, Motor sports, especially competitive Hill Climbs and Formula 1, investigating paranormal activities, classic car rebuilds (Completed Lamborghini Countach and AC Cobra.) Participating as team member in snooker matches.

ADDITIONAL INFORMATION

Full clean driving licence

References available upon request.

SIMON JACKSON
Flat 18, Derby Hall
Wimbledon Road
Bournemouth BH7 6HW
Tel: 01111 111111   Mob: 00000 000000
E-mail: simonjacks@hotmail.co.uk

SKILLS PROFILE

- A highly motivated professional with extensive business management experience within the licensed sector, establishing new clubs, pubs and family orientated bar/restaurants.
- First class business, sales, marketing and financial management skills, achieving objectives through innovation, team motivation and strong leadership.
- Organising, promoting and developing theme/event nights, consistently achieving and surpassing target revenues.
- Reactive to change, proactive to challenge and performance driven.
- Ideally suited to exploiting above key skills within business management, marketing or similar demanding work environment.

EMPLOYMENT HISTORY

2004-2006   **General Manager,**
Gardenias (Trading as The Countryman), Blandford, Dorset.
Responsible for establishing a busy town centre bar, recognised as one of the main student clubs, substantially increasing turnover.

2001-2004   **General Manager.**
Bat & Ball, Blandford, Dorset.
Involved from the initial stages in establishing Blandford's only rooftop terrace restaurant and bar, increasing turnover to in excess of £1m per annum, introducing specialist nights and entertainment programmes, gaining an award as one of the South's best new bars.

2000-2001   **General Manager.**
Barnaby's, Blandfor, Dorset.
Involved in the opening of a new town centre venue catering for the older person, incorporating a choice of three menus, cool sophisticated music and a lively bar.

2000-2000   **General Manager.**
CCC Restaurants, (Blanford Branch), Dorset.
Completing a short-term contract for a Reading based company, managing a busy Italian pizza/pasta restaurant. Increasing revenue from £9K to £18K through improved customer service and standards.

1996-1999   **Manager.**
Dougall and Bashley Catering, Barton-on-Sea, Hampshire..
Responsible for the management of a two hundred cover restaurant and four bars, with additional facilities catering for up to seventy children. Dramatically increasing turn over, catering for between 500-600 people per day.

CAREER SUMMARY

Additional employment would include working within the licensed/hospitality sector as a Relief & Holding Manager, travelling throughout the country covering 38 different establishments. Further experience as a Trainee Manager at a newly established outlet 'The Gables,' a 130 seat restaurant with a turnover of 30K per week, developing a solid skills base in all aspects of business management.

EDUCATION, ACHIEVEMENTS AND ADDITIONAL TRAINING EXPERIENCE

National Certificate for Entertainment Licences (NCEL)

BIIAB level 11 – Door Supervisors – Gold Card
(Modules)
NCDS Stage 1, Drugs Awareness & Fire Safety, Conflict Management, Physical Intervention
First Aid

Training Courses
Leadership & Motivation Advanced – Basic & Intermediate levels of Food Hygiene
First Aid – HASAWA & COSHH

'O' level in eight subjects including Maths and English, 'A' level in Technical Drawing

LEISURE INTERESTS

Enjoy keeping up to date on current affairs, listening to a wide range of music, travelling and cinema.

ADDITIONAL INFORMATION

Clean Current Driving Licence

References Available upon Request

VIVIAN COLE
442 Ashley Road
Bournemouth BH1 1PP
Tel: 01202 123456

SKILLS PROFILE

- **A highly motivated, focused administrator familiar with all systems and procedures of a busy office environment.**
- **Responsible for direct client liaison, audio typing, data entry, diary management, report compilations and all day to day office requirements.**
- **Further experience gained within both the retail and financial sectors including stock controls, customer services, cash handling, accounting, promotions, security and direct sales.**
- **Used to working within high-pressure environments where initiative and logic are prime requisites, demonstrating well proven communication and customer care skills.**
- **Ideally seeking a position where above skills and experiences could be drawn upon and further developed, preferably as a legal secretary or similar role.**

QUALIFICATIONS

RSA Typewriting – Stage 1 (Distinction)
RSA Word Processing – Stage 1, Part 2 (Distinction)
RSA Word Processing – Stage 2, Part 2 (Distinction)
RSA Text Processing – Stage 1, Part 1 (Distinction)
RSA Text Processing – Stage 1, Part 2 (Distinction)
Ilex (Paralegal Training)
Legal Secretary – Level 3 (Diploma Merit)

Computer Literate (Windows 2000, Word Perfect 5.2) CLAIT

(Currently studying Legal Text Processing and 'A' level Business Studies)

EDUCATION

King William School, Somerset
Educated to GCE standards including 'O' level Business Studies

Bushwater College, Somerset
GCSE 'A' level – Law

CAREER SUMMARY

Retail Assistant. Eves Childs Wear, Bridgewater, Somerset.
Working within a busy shop environment, serving customers, stock controls, cash handling, basic bookkeeping and banking.

Cashier. Abbey National Building Society, Burridge-on-Sea.
Direct public liaison, advising on investments and mortgages, telephone inquiries, cheque and cash handling, all administrative procedures.

LEISURE INTERESTS

Enjoy keeping fit (Member of local Health Club), weightlifting, going for long beach and countryside walks, cooking, reading a wide range of literature and all aspects of interior design.

ADDITIONAL INFORMATION

Clean Current Driving Licence

References Available upon Request

LETTERS

The following letter writing examples are broken down into two categories.

A. The Speculative approach

This letter is normally sent to employers asking about any potential vacancies that exist or positions that may become available. Usually this form of letter accompanies a CV/Résumé.

B. The advertised response

This form of letter is a direct response to an advertisement and is tailored towards the position.

The examples are easily interchangeable and can be arranged according to your particular requirements. By borrowing a line from here or a paragraph from there you will quickly be able to come up with the perfect letter to accompany your CV/Résumé.

EXAMPLES
OF
SPECULATIVE
LETTERS

Martin King
Apartment 4A
West Drive
Brighton
E. Sussex
BT12 8TT
Tel: (01202)111111

Fao: Mr. D. Williams
Meredith Business Development
66 The Rubicon
Portsmouth
Hampshire
PO5 6NQ

25th November 2006

Dear Mr. Williams,

Ref: Employment Opportunities

I am interested in developing my career in public house/club management having gained five years experience in supervisory positions within the food and beverage industry.

My CV will demonstrate success in organising and developing business initiatives as well as the day-to-day supervision of all functions/activities. I am also acknowledged for leading motivating staff members to work to their maximum performance, adopting a lively, energetic approach to new ideas and challenges.

I would welcome the opportunity of an interview regarding any training or supervisory positions, where I am sure my enthusiasm and credibility will not leave you unimpressed.

Yours sincerely,

Martin King

Fred Bloggs
9 Dudsbury Crescent
Winton
Bournemouth
BH8 8NS
Tel: (01202) 222222

Fao: Mr. V. James (Personnel Manager)
Meridian Technology Plc.
Unit 7-9
Wetstone Business Park
Bournemouth
BH19 9DD

12th December 2006

Dear Mr. James,

On hearing that your company is undergoing an expansion program, I decided it may be to our mutual benefit that I bring my background in production management to your attention.

I have enclosed my CV, which details substantial achievements within major companies both in systems improvements and the resultant cost benefits. Of further interest to you will be the valuable network of UK and international contacts I have built throughout my career, which offer further opportunities for development.

I understand your management team is likely to be in place, nevertheless if you do identify opportunities in which I could compliment your team, I would be pleased to hear of them. In the meantime I welcome your response.

Yours sincerely,

Fred Bloggs

Jennifer Eccles
215 Sea View Road
Boscombe
Bournemouth
BH4 4FG
Tel: 01202 111222

Fao: Human Resources
Alfred Thames Limited
1009 Sedgemoor Road
Bournemouth
BH1 6FL

19th October 2006

Dear Sir,

Having had over six years experience in cashiering and two years as a post room clerk, I am writing to discover if your company has any similar positions where my skills could be put to good use.

My enclosed CV details my responsibilities and competence with this type of work and also my proficiency with basic computer skills.

You will find I am a punctual, loyal employee who always gives one hundred percent commitment and any opportunities available would be well received.

In the meantime I look forward to your response.

Yours faithfully,

Jennifer Eccles

Janet Bailey
90 South West Drive
Southbourne
Bournemouth
BH5 2LK
Tel: 01202 000000

Blueprint Communications
Commercial Road
Bournemouth
BH1 1PR   3rd January 2007

Dear Sir,

I write to you as a first step in exploring the possibility of employment with your company as an installation engineer.

My CV is enclosed which details my work experience, hitherto as you can see, I have four years experience in Telecommunications working for a company which dealt in various private branch exchange systems.

When I first joined TMB Systems, I had no previous knowledge what so ever of telephone systems but quickly learnt and adapted to the position, one of my strengths. This demonstrates my ability to learn and during my period of employment with TNB worked on many systems including the Mitel range – SX20, SX50, SX200 and Meridian Norstar.

I am enthusiastic, capable of working as part of a team or on my own, accurate, meticulous and good at problem solving. I enjoy dealing with people and have a good sense of fun, but I am serious about my responsibilities. I believe that I would certainly be a valuable asset to any company.

The opportunity of an interview would be well received where I am sure my enthusiasm would become readily apparent.

Thank you for your time.

Yours faithfully,

Janet Bailey

Simon Bartlett
41 Asprey Gardens
Winton
Bournemouth
BH9 6EE
Tel: (01202)000000

Spencers Stores Limited
Castle Point
Castle Lane
Bournemouth
BH3 16YG

9th September 2006

Dear Sir,

Having gained experience within the fast food industry, I am enquiring to see if you have any retail assistant vacancies in your company.

You will find my CV enclosed as evidence of my suitability. I have good customer service skills and interact well with the public, also quick and accurate skills in cash handling and can be relied upon for my punctuality with hard work.

Having a sense of humour and the ability to communicate well with other members of staff, I know that should an interview become available, I would be able to show my enthusiasm and with that in mind I will phone you within the next few days.

Yours faithfully,

Simon Bartlett

Paul Hook
22 Wellfield Avenue
Moordown
Bournemouth
BH3 3KH
Tel: 00000 000000

The Manager
Highgate Motors
988 Valley Road
Bournemouth
BH2 12NB   4th January 2007

Dear Sir,

I am approaching your company with a view to employment as a trainee
motor mechanic and would be pleased to learn of any such
apprenticeships you may be able to offer me.

My experience is limited to working for friends and family but it may
interest you to know that I am capable of stripping down/replacing parts,
repairing bodywork and locating electrical faults.

As an eighteen year old I am obviously seeking a structured career and
you can be assured of 100% commitment, punctuality and reliability.

If you do foresee any such opportunities I would be pleased to hear of
them, in the meantime I welcome your response and advice.

Yours faithfully,

Paul Hook

David McGovern
Flat C
121 Aylesbury Road
Bournemouth
BH1 4NG
Tel: 00000 000000

Personnel Manager
Crystal Design
18-48 Carlton Road
Bournemouth
BH1 9TF

19th December 2006

Dear Sir,

Having recently visited your shop I was so impressed that I decided to write to enquire about joining your sales team.

I have a wealth of retail experience including positions of trust within the diamond cutting industry, demonstrating the ability to work within a team or on my own initiative.

You would find me a very useful member of staff, having an artistic flair with a keen eye for display areas. I would be ideally suited in this type of store. I have enclosed a copy of my CV, which I hope you find of interest.

I look forward to hearing from you in anticipation of an interview.

Yours faithfully,

David McGovern

Brian Goody
112a South Kinson Drive
Bournemouth
BH4 5NK
Tel: 00000 111111

Personnel Manager
Elstree Logistics
1009 Wallisdown Road
Poole
BH12 3JL   10th October 2006

Dear Sir,

I would like to enquire if you have any vacancies in your stores or goods inward department.

My enclosed Curriculum Vitae details my employment history showing that I have extensive experience, carrying out all warehouse/storekeepers duties including checking damaged goods and stocktaking. During my previous employment I gained qualifications as a high-reach truck operator to unload lorries and stack stock.

Recently I completed courses at Bournemouth International Airport to become a certified counter balance operator and gain computer skills, enabling me to contribute and keep up with new technology. I have always considered myself as hardworking, sensible, quiet and reliable but above all else you will find me loyal.

I would like to join you because I know I have the experience you require. I accept that you may not as yet have any vacancies but would like to be considered for any in the near future.

I look forward to hearing from you soon.

Yours faithfully,

Brian Goody

Jenny Bryant
78 Old Farmhouse Lane
New Milton
Hampshire
BH26 19SB
Tel: 00000 222222

The Personnel Manager
Crosskey Services & Design Studio
24-27 High Street
Basingstoke
Hampshire

Dear Sir,   19th July 2006

Re: Part Time Sales Assistant

I was very interested to read of your company's intention of opening up a new branch in New Milton and would like to apply for one of your part-time assistant positions.

My background in catering resulted in the achievement of responsible positions, where first class customer service was of paramount importance to maintain and increase revenue. I believe it is important to listen carefully to the customer and advise accordingly, whilst maintaining a friendly and approachable disposition, these are just some of the skills I would bring to the position. Of further interest to you will be a lively interest in interior design, arts and craft, covering a wide range of products and styles.

The rewards for my commitment to the position I would see at around £5 per hour with prospects for future advancement based on performance.

I would welcome the opportunity to expand on my value at interview and in the meantime look forward to your response.

Yours faithfully,

Jenny Bryant

Martin Shearer
Flat 9
2 Bracken Road
Christchurch
BH25 8UH
Tel: 11111 111111

Fao: Mr. P. Sykes (Site Foreman)
Westland Construction
Unit 8-12
Ferndown Industrial Estate
BH 22 6KC   17th August 2006

Dear Mr. Sykes,

As a young man trying to get into the building industry I am writing to find out whether you may need a trainee.

Although most of my experience has been in other industries, I have done quite a bit of labouring for friends and family. I am hoping to begin formal training soon (On my own time) but really feel that the best experience I could get would be 'On the job.'

Should the above be of interest to you, I would welcome the opportunity for an interview where I am sure you would not be disappointed. In the meantime I look forward to your response.

Yours sincerely,

Martin Shearer

Miss S. Brown
2 Parisian Walk
Newcastle
SA2 1AZ
Tel: 001 234599

FAO: Mr. Jackson
Kenwood Offices
The Grange
Unit 4
51 Faulkner Street
Tyneside
NW14 2AA

14th August 2006

Dear Mr. Jackson,

I am writing to explore the prospects of any administrative positions that may be available within your company and enclose my CV as evidence of my suitability.

Briefly, I have kept myself up-to-date with developments in the industry, including successive budget changes.

You will find me not only a personable and co-operative individual thoroughly rehearsed in the mechanic and presentation of a professional office environment, but also quick to adopt new systems and procedures.

The opportunity of an interview to discuss any possible openings would be most welcome and I look forward to your response.

Yours sincerely,

Susan Brown

Phillip Hiden
1386 Uphill Walk
Downton
DO3 1KP
Tel: 010009 390312

FAO: Personnel Department
Paperchase
2 Edward Street
Kingston
London
NW1 6AA

17th June 2006

Dear Sir/Madam,

I am writing to register my interest in working for your company as a Portfolio Technician and enclose my CV in support of my application.

Briefly, having completed parts I, II and III of the F.P.C. I am now keen to fully exploit my skills and knowledge (particularly of the stock market) to help manage portfolio investment. Although I have limited work experience, my skills and motivation dictate I would quickly fit in with your systems, procedures and training.

Opportunities are hard to come by in a highly competitive marketplace but if you believe, as I do, that we have a basis for further discussion, I would be pleased to hear from you. In the meantime I welcome your response.

Yours faithfully,

Phillip Hiden

Brenda Goode
5 Freeze Street
Bristol
BA11 2FF

Mr. A. Symmons
Symmons & Son Estate Agents
Friary Lane
Witheridge
EX1 6PP

2nd February 2007

Dear Sirs,

I write to enquire of any vacancies you may have for an administrator with a wealth of experience in both retail and office environments.

As the enclosed CV details, I have a solid background of administrative experience combined with a number of teaching qualifications which I believe prove my ability to communicate effectively at all levels. In addition I am fully computer literate with an understanding of a variety of packages (Word, Works, Office etc). My experience has also enabled me to further refine my bookkeeping knowledge. As the sole proprietor of a retail outlet I have found that my organisational and time-management skills are highly developed.

I can guarantee complete commitment and reliability, along with a practical and realistic approach to all tasks issued. With a background of customer service I fully understand the importance of presenting a professional image at all times.

The opportunity to discuss this further at interview would be most welcome and I am available on the number given above at any time.

Yours faithfully,

Brenda Goode (Miss)

ADVERTISED

RESPONSE

LETTERS

Mike Powers
224 North Ridge
Parkstone
Dorset
BH19 4KT
Tel: 01202 444444

Daniel Rickardo
C.C. Design & Production Limited
Morecombe House
Bournemouth International Airport
Dorset
BH23 5NH

23rd August 2006

Dear Mr. Rickardo,

Re: Vacancy for Area Sales Manager

I was interested to learn of your vacancy for an Area Sales Manager and I believe I offer the required combination of experience, knowledge and skills to become a valued team member.

My experience has included selling high end user quality kitchens to both domestic and commercial sectors of the market, developing sound business relationships thus ensuring repeat business. I have been consistently recognised for meeting and exceeding ambitious company sales and quality targets, whilst providing first class customer service.

Fundamental to my success is the powerful combination of sales ability, IT skills and a thorough understanding of the builder/developer market place, I believe my enthusiasm and commitment for the position would become evident at interview. In the meantime I look forward to hearing from you.

Yours sincerely,

Mike Powers

Philip Ingram
196 Aylesbury Road
Bournemouth
BH1 4HY
Tel: 01202 222222

The Chairman
Bournemouth Athletics Club
114 Fairfield Road
West Parley
BH23 5GH

17th December 2006

Dear Sir,

I was interested to read of your advertisement for a club manager and have enclosed my Curriculum Vitae as evidence of my success to date.

My management ability has developed well through a combination of focus, innovation and initiative. Whilst with my previous company revenue increased twenty fold, a result of more effective merchandising, ambitious sales targets, motivation and regular training initiatives. The prospect of applying these key skills to your own development programme is a stimulating one and one which would demand professional marketing skills to attract new business. My experience with events and catering management would undoubtedly add weight to these objectives.

It should also be said I have a strong sporting background in competitive swimming, rugby, netball and currently referee for local football and rugby teams.

In short, the experience and knowledge are in place, the management skills have been well-tested and I believe my enthusiasm for the position would become evident at interview.

Yours faithfully,

Philip Ingram

Mark Browning
3 Penby Gardens
Poole BH18 8YY
Tel: 00000 000000

Peter Davis Limited
High Street
Poole
BH18 4SX

12th December 2006

Ref: Assistant Manager

Dear Mr. Davis,

Your recent advertisement regarding the above position interested me for a number of reasons which may be summarised as follows:

Experience

Seven years with 'Watches of Switzerland' involving selling prestige branded watches and accessories to a discerning client base. Achieved five consecutive monthly awards for 'Sales excellence,' and awarded promotion to sales supervisor.

Attitude

Pro-active and professional with a keen interest in market trends and evaluation. A 'hands on' supervisor who is client-led and who believes strongly in quality and presentation. Aspirations towards full management via a structured and meaningful career path. Determined to achieve these aims through hard work and attention to detail.

Knowledge

Comprehensive knowledge of the jewellery market including metal, stones, engraving, cutting, design and manufacture.

Finally, I am more than aware of the Peter Davis commitment towards staff development and training, I believe my career to date would act as a valuable springboard in becoming an effective assistant manager with your company. I believe an interview would meet both our requirements and I welcome your response.

Yours sincerely

Mark Browning

David Downing
98 Alder Road
Parkstone
BH19 9LK
Tel: 00000 111111

Fao: Mr. Terry Bailey
Langtry Hostel
77 Suffolk Road
Bournemouth BH1 2JT

10th January 2007

Ref: Hostel Manager

Dear Mr. Bailey,

Having enjoyed a substantial amount of responsibility within the hotel and leisure industry (To management level), I am now in a position to fully exploit my experience.

Briefly, my CV demonstrates restaurant and banqueting experience gained both in the UK and overseas. I have worked in five star hotels leading teams of up to three hundred for important functions and clients. My success in this area has been acknowledged as professional and is well documented on my CV.

Finally, I believe I have much to offer your company. My expectations are realistic, my standards and communication skills have been well developed.

An interview would be welcome when I am confident my enthusiasm will not leave you unimpressed.

Yours sincerely

David Downing

John Wellman
62 The Grove
Bournemouth
BH3 9LN

Mr. J. Goody (General Manager)
Salisbury Cathedral
Salisbury
SP1 2EN   10th August 2006

<u>Ref: Works Manager</u>

Dear Mr. Goody,

I am eager to join your team in the above capacity and offer my Curriculum Vitae as evidence of my credibility.

Briefly it will demonstrate proven man-management skills within a large multi-site working environment.

With over thirty years experience in the Civil Engineering/Construction industries, including restructuring and refurbishment programmes, being clearly focused on delegating responsibilities and defining projects in hand, I would be confident of fulfilling the job criteria.

The need for clear communication skills are paramount in dealing with not only internal forces but external organisations, in adhering to strict Health/Safety procedures and project management issues, are just some of the qualities I would bring to the position.

To augment my practical skills my remit also includes The Diploma in Business Management, City & Guilds 11 in quantities and estimating with a working knowledge of Joint Contract Trades contracting.

The Salisbury project particularly stimulates me and I believe my ability would offer a valuable contribution towards the efficiency and ultimate success of the improvement programme.

I look forward to your reply.

Yours sincerely

John Wellman

Maria Gold
14C Carlton Towers
Poole
Dorset
BH19 4RJ
Tel: 01202 555555

Mrs. K Denton
P.O. Box 119
Mortimer
RG7 9OK

12th December 2006

Ref: Administrative Secretary

Dear Mrs. Denton,

I am interested in joining your team in the post of Administrative Secretary and enclose my CV, which should demonstrate my capability for producing a high standard of work.

My experience has largely been gained with Paultons Solicitors as P.A. to the Senior Partner. My responsibilities included reception work, telephone liaison, word processing, mail sorting and diary management. Being a busy practice there were inevitably periods of pressure but having developed good time management skills, I learnt the importance of initiative, maintaining a pleasant helpful manner with both clients and colleagues.

Finally, I am pleased you welcome applications from more mature candidates, because at forty-six I believe I have a great deal of experience to offer your company and the opportunity of an interview would give me a chance to prove this to you.

Yours sincerely,

Maria Gold

Matthew Kelly
24 Wimborne Crescent
Poole
BH15 9EW
Tel: 01202 555555

Mr. Nick Larson
Field Personnel Manager
Grays Traffic Controls Ltd.
Poole
BH17 9EY   16th September 2006

Ref: Health & Safety Manager

Dear Mr. Larson,

I am interested in applying for the above position and believe I offer the necessary level of skills and experience to become successful in the role.

Briefly, my CV demonstrates over eight years experience embracing all factors relevant to Health & Safety issues. My technical training has enabled me not only to identify areas of improvement, but also the capability to effectively communicate solutions throughout the workforce. I also place great importance on monitoring progress and introducing training initiatives on a regular basis, in order to maintain awareness and promote efficiency.

You will find me a professional, logical and astute individual who is always willing to contribute to the team effort, bringing added value to the position whenever necessary.

The opportunity of an interview would be welcome when I am confident my enthusiasm for the position will soon become apparent.

In the meantime I look forward to your response.

Yours sincerely,

Matthew Kelly

Tammy Fielding
'The Willows'
18 Glen Road
Bournemouth
BH2 4PL
Tel: (01202) 888888

Mr. Jacobs,
Abbott Menswear
77 Westover Road
Bournemouth
BH1 9UU   14th December 2006

Dear Mr. Jacobs,

I was interested to learn of your vacancy for a sales assistant and have enclosed my CV as evidence of my suitability.

Briefly, my CV indicates retail experience as well as catering and bar work. Both positions required me to deliver a good standard of customer service if repeat orders were to be achieved. I have also developed good cash handling skills and can be relied upon for my punctuality, hard work and accuracy.

Finally, I have a lively personality and take a keen interest in both male and female fashions.

The opportunity of an interview would be well received when I am sure my enthusiasm for the position will quickly become apparent.

In the meantime I look forward to your response.

Yours sincerely,

Tammy Fielding

Anthony Hisslop
12a Bingley Road
Bournemouth
BH1 3IG
Tel: 01202 888777

GEX Communications Agency
Unit 19-23
Goring Business Park
West Parley
Poole
BH23 7TS

19th July 2006

Ref: European Sales Managers

Dear Sir,

I was interested to read of your advertisement for the above position and have enclosed my CV as evidence of my experience and credibility to date.

Briefly, it will demonstrate a relevant combination of OEM/ATE sales experience in the UK, Europe, USA and Pacific Rim in the avionics, mobile communication and PCB assembly market.

It is this combination which I believe will be of particular interest to you. In addition to this my work in market/product development reinforced with excellent relationship skills would undoubtedly add strength to your clients company.

The ATE experience is in place, the personal qualities have been well tested and I believe my enthusiasm for this position would become evident at interview.

Yours faithfully,

Anthony Hisslop

Robert Teller
1009 Talbot Avenue
Branksome
Poole
BH14 6DP
Tel: (01202) 111111

Mr. David DuPont
DuPont Advertising
28-30 West Canford Drive
Bournemouth
BII4 4YG

20th September 2006

<u>Ref: Territory Manager</u>

Dear Mr. DuPont,

I am very interested in applying for the above position and offer my CV as evidence of my suitability and success to date.

My experience appears to closely match your specification for the position. As a sales manager at Ravlon it was necessary to be a good communicator and focused on the achievement of sales goals.

As I understand it the position required a self-motivated customer approach with the necessary interpersonal skills. My sales skills have been achieved over a number of years in a very competitive market place. I have a flexible and outgoing personality.

The opportunity to expand on what I am able to offer at interview would be welcome when I am confident my enthusiasm will become apparent.

Yours sincerely,

Robert Teller

Andrew Caldicott
21 Dean Gardens
Bournemouth
BH1 3JJ
Tel: 01202 444444

Mrs. Linda Josephs
Hilton-Brant International
25 Long Acre Walk
Farnham GU9 8HK

19th July 2006

Dear Mrs. Josephs,

Re: General Manager Ref: 1127-7YT1E

Following your recent advertisement for the above vacancy on the Internet JobSite Vacancy Service. I would like to offer my CV as evidence of my credibility for the position and my success to date.

The position calls for a successful track record in corporate management and finance, project management, health & safety/quality assurance of a young growth company in the property services sector. Perhaps the following achievement examples will indicate my suitability for this key management role.

- Successfully started-up a facilities project management and engineering consultancy business with responsibility for control of all aspects of the company including finance.
- Project leadership of a £38m facilities refurbishment for Meltis Inc (offices, laboratories and manufacturing maintained fully operational) including health & safety, cost control, QA/validation.
- 13 years business development experience at senior level in BACC plc building services and facilities management company Hopper Young Limited.

I believe my experience and exposure to all disciplines in the property services sector would fully meet the demands of the position. The opportunity to expand further on the benefits I have to offer would be welcome. In the meantime I look forward to your response.

Yours sincerely

Andrew Caldicott

James Barton
93 East Downton Road
Basingstoke
RG15 8NM
Tel: 00000 000000

Mr. Edward Woolam
Elskin Laboratory Products
P.O. Box 2909
Basingstoke
RG22 9IO   10th August 2006

Dear Mr. Woolam,

Having recently been made redundant from my position as warehouse person with Crawley Opticals of Basingstoke, I was very pleased to learn of your vacancy as your requirements appear to closely match my own experience.

My responsibilities included the loading and checking of deliveries, careful handling and packing of orders for despatch. I also offer a current fork-lift licence covering both reach and counter balance, plus a clean driving licence should I be called upon for relief driving.

Finally, I completed a CLAIT course in September 2002 and have good basic computer skills. I live locally and have only been off work twice in over three years, so you may be assured of my reliability.

The opportunity of an interview would be welcome where I would be pleased to discuss the position in more detail. In the meantime I look forward to your response.

Yours sincerely,

James Barton

Martin Sweep
221 Tadley Common Road
Basingstoke
RG25 6TY
Tel: 00000 000000

Ms. D. Zeledon
Personnel Department
College of Air Traffic Controls
Christchurch
BH23 9GH

22nd November 2006

Dear Ms. Zeledon,

Re: SIMULATOR OPERATOR

I am interested in joining your team in the above position and enclose my CV as evidence of my credibility.

My career to date appears to closely match the requirements of the position and may be summarised as follows:

AVIATION EXPERIENCE: My work with Christchurch Flying Club as operations co-ordinator involved the scheduling of available aircraft with instructors/student pilots. Prior experience to this was with the RAF undertaking various tasks for military photo reconnaissance. It may be of further interest to you that I also hold a private pilot's licence.

MANUAL DEXTERITY: Whilst with the RAF my work involved the processing and developing of film as well as the loading of camera equipment to a variety of aircraft types.

COMMUNICATION SKILLS; As a driving school proprietor and sales director I was responsible for designing and presenting training programmes to gain measured results, liaising with a team of ten instructors and two secretaries.

COMPETENT I.T. SKILLS: Familiar with P.C's and programmes such as 'Flite Sim' and 'Tracon 11.' Worked with computerised monitoring systems at Soya Marine Engines for endurance testing of pre-production engines.

AVIATION STUDIES: An intensive course at London Guildhall University in both the navigation and technical elements of the commercial pilots licence ground examinations.

The aviation experience is in place, the personal qualities have been well tested and I believe my enthusiasm for the position would become evident at interview.

I welcome your reply,

Yours sincerely,

Martin Sweep

Martin Shaw
The Old School House
School Lane
Fordingbridge
Hampshire
FN2 7PC

Ms. Brenda Rawe
Personnel Department
London Victoria Society
Fosgate House
Clapham
London
EC1 5PP

17th June 2006

Dear Ms. Rawe,

RE: Vacancy for Treasury Assistant

I am eager to join your team in the above capacity and believe I Hold the necessary experience and personal qualities to become successful in the position.

Briefly as outlined in my Curriculum Vitae my work with Charlton Masey involved many of the responsibilities you outline in your advertisement. Included amongst these were responsibilities for CHAPS payments and other transfers, funding and deposit positioning to treasury dealers and all forms of cash management procedures.

You will find me a flexible individual, capable of an efficient and focused approach to work, quick to learn new procedures and integrate with the team.

The opportunity of an interview would be welcome and I look forward to your reply.

Yours sincerely,

Martin Shaw

Peter Daniels
219 Old Holborn Road
Christchurch
BH25 7MM

James & Stewart Accountants
17 Poole Lane
Wimborne
BH22 19OP

20th January 2007

Re: The next piece in your jigsaw

Dear Sir,

Your jigsaws not complete
Mine is not too
Therefore let us meet
And see what we can do.

Briefly my career history has encompassed the full remit of financial accounting and technical skills including the tax regimes, PAYE, NI and VAT that you mention.

As a qualified accountant I have achieved the commercial recognition expected from leading companies and certainly am able to offer, a valuable mix of skills and understanding that relates to wide-ranging business needs. I also believe strongly in the value of business partnerships with clients, offering the commercial perspectives which bring added value to clients objectives.

My CV outlines the key experience, but perhaps more importantly, the offer of an interview will allow me to tell you how in more detail I could address the imbalance in your team and complete your matrix.

Of further interest to you will be the fact that I live locally where travel to Wimborne will not be a problem. I can also be flexible regarding the days required, either part-time or full, or whatever you feel your jigsaw requires.

I welcome your response,

Peter Daniels

Printed in the United Kingdom
by Lightning Source UK Ltd.
123349UK00003B/1/A